A Primer on the
ECONOMIC HISTORY
of EUROPE

A Primer on

The Primer series is under the editorial ∾∾∾∾∾∾
supervision of PETER L. BERNSTEIN

the ECONOMIC HISTORY *of* EUROPE

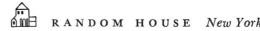 Paul Hohenberg

Cornell University

RANDOM HOUSE   *New York*

For J.

1473992

Preface

The function of a preface is twofold. It is supposed to inform the reader about the scope and content of the book and to acknowledge the intellectual debts incurred by the author in writing it. I propose, instead, to concentrate on what the book omits and to indicate the shortcomings in the work of others that led me to undertake it.

To deal first with the latter point. As a teacher I have found myself perplexed in trying to put together a bibliography for students desiring only a genteel sufficiency of European economic history, let alone in recommending something for the general reader. Particular aspects of the subject are brilliantly dealt with, sometimes in concise and readable form, but there are great gaps. Past syntheses, on the other hand, have tended to enlist the historical record in the service of an a priori idea or cause. This *Primer* is a modest effort at bringing the longer perspective of European history to bear on the justly popular problem of economic growth. I am aware that it is incomplete, although I know too well the critical faculties of my fellow economic historians to suppose that no one can be more conscious than myself of the book's shortcomings.

In the interests of brevity, perspective, and focus, I have left out a great many things one would ordinarily associate with economic history. There is virtually no treatment of economic ideas beyond a mention or two of Adam Smith, Marx, and Keynes, and something about the mercantile and scholastic doctrines. Institutional forms have been slighted, and episodes made famous by their violent or spectacular nature even more so. There is less about the Rothschilds, even, than about banking techniques, and I deal no more with massacres of rebellious peasants and striking workers than with the organization of labor unions. Finally, scholars may wonder at the short shrift given many of their favorite debates. On reflection, I find that the literature tends to emphasize topics convenient to deal with at the expense of inherently more critical matters. As the late Paul Baran used to say, we teach—and study—what we can analyze elegantly rather than what is important to know. I have devoted the space gained by these omissions to more detailed coverage of preindustrial Europe than is usual.

My intellectual debts are, of course, considerable. The greatest and most obvious is to the company of scholars from whose writings the entire book is drawn, almost always without acknowledgment. I hope that their work has not suffered severe distortion in the strenuous process of selection, compression, and synthesis. I should also mention my students, who have provided a responsive sounding board for ideas and ways of presenting them. More directly, I am indebted to the Series editor, Peter L. Bernstein, for constant encouragement and incisive stylistic help, although I assume full responsibility for errors of substance. Miss Julie Roemer and Miss Monique Chaumet typed drafts of the manuscript with good-humored efficiency.

Finally, let me acknowledge a particular debt to my subject— to Europe, where the book was written. Being there has made me aware of continuing past roots as well as onrushing present change in European life, and also of the extent to which human labor and ingenuity have molded—as they are now remolding—the landscapes and the cultures of the Continent. Yet I have learned something about myself as well, about my own intellectual biases in approaching economic history. The book is steeped in the bourgeois Anglo-Saxon tradition of American economics. I do not apologize for the fact, but venture to hope that this is a better book for my heightened awareness of other methods and points of view.

Stanford, California   PAUL HOHENBERG
January, 1968

Contents

A Primer on the
ECONOMIC HISTORY
of EUROPE

Introduction

Why study economic history? In many ways, economic history is the epitome of dry, scholarly, and tedious anti-quarianism. Not that earning a living or the quest for wealth have lacked drama, romance, and violence. But it is fair to warn the reader that we shall give little emphasis to glorious and gory episodes, to the heroes and villains of commerce, industry, and finance, except sometimes to recall favorite legends in order to debunk them. On the contrary, we shall insist on the continuity of economic activity made necessary by the need for every man to secure each day his daily bread. No matter how dark the age, there had to be food for most people most of the time, or their society would not have survived. On the other hand, the most glorious discoveries and inventions were only imperceptible nudges along the weary and still incomplete journey of mankind toward freedom from Adam's curse. In the richest cities, the bulk of the population has always lived very near the limit of subsistence, while disaster or stealthy erosion through economic change stalked even legendary wealth.

Even for those who do not yearn to know every detail of the Irish linen-weaving industry of the eighteenth century, economic history can yield a good measure of fun. It offers us glimpses of the past in its everyday clothes, instead of its ceremonial best. This informal look helps provide much-needed perspective. It is, I think, of particular interest to those who have a running acquaintance with the past from what are now curiously called books of history. History of what? Voltaire once said that history was no more than the portrayal of crimes and tragic events. He may have been pessimistic about mankind when he said this, but it can equally well be taken as a criticism of the work of historians. They have tended to emphasize the unique event, the colorful character, the sensational, the brutal, the glamorous. One might say that history, and schoolbook history in particular, is the yellow journalism of the past. A contemporary philosopher, Karl Popper, has blamed historians for emphasizing what he calls "the history of international crime and mass murder." The economic historian prefers to write the back pages of mythical newspapers of the past. How people lived and worked, the movement of goods, the motives for great enterprises and many lesser ones, the attitudes and rules governing work, thrift, risk, and novelty—these are his concern. And one can argue that this perspective is perhaps more fruitful in understanding the past than the study of battles, treaties, and even revolutions. Is France not more truly reflected in carefully tended vineyards than in apocryphal stories of Joan of Arc and Robespierre, and England in her traders and cotton men rather than in Robin Hood and Lord Nelson?

Indeed, we can do more than reconstruct the economic past and compensate for our inability to experience it directly. With the powerful tools of economic theory and with modern techniques of historiography and statistical analysis, we can form a picture of past societies far more complete and sophisticated than was available to any contemporaries.

We know which of their dreams and worries materialized, and which were illusory, partly through hindsight, but largely because we now have better sources of information about the past than were available to contemporaries. Finally, we can ask questions they never even thought of, and thus integrate into our picture of the times phenomena that troubled contemporaries or escaped them entirely for long periods.

Of course, we too are prisoners of ignorance and victims of our cultural blinders, but man has progressed in his peculiarly characteristic ability to examine his own affairs, if not always to manage them.

Yet the reader is well entitled to expect a justification of our subject in terms of understanding the present and preparing for the future. It is not my intention to add to the venerable debate about the uses of history. Economic history is not, I think, without its lessons, even for those who shy away from the kind of grandiose determinism that Karl Marx brilliantly distilled from his study of economic change. But it is for each student to draw his own lessons. My own modest conclusions will peep out here and there.

In order to have any hope of compressing the rich diversity of our story into a few pages without dehydrating it completely, it is necessary to adopt a point of view, and one can hardly do otherwise than choose one appropriate to our time. Here the stress will be on the theme of economic growth, that is, the increase over time of the amount of goods and services to which the inhabitants of an economy —local, regional, and especially national—have access. We cannot totally ignore other goals and values, such as freedom, variety, and equity, but they will be subordinated to the main theme. Other choices were possible. We might have related economic life and change to noneconomic ends, to their effects on cultural life or on the development of political and social relations. Because we have not done so, it should not be inferred that economic goals are considered primary and others less important.

Finally, a warning: The subject is vast, and the present

format, as well as our knowledge, sharply limited. The synthesizer rushes in where specialists fear to tread. Let the reader himself add the qualifications and doubts. He should amend most of the statements that follow, scattering a host of mental "sometimeses," "hardly evers," "probablys," "so-far-as-we-knows," and other verbal grains of salt. One admission can be made explicitly here. When we speak of Europe, we often will be speaking only of Western Europe, that is, of what are now Britain, France, Germany, Northern Italy, and the Low Countries. Russia, Scandinavia, the Mediterranean regions, and the Balkans will receive inadequate attention from time to time.

PART I

PREINDUSTRIAL EUROPE

CHAPTER 1

The Concept of
an Economic Surplus

At several points in our narrative, we shall pause briefly to introduce and comment on a useful economic concept. This is not intended to compete either with the learned authors of the other Primers in this series or with textbook writers. It is merely a convenient way of agreeing on some common language.

The economic surplus is that part of any economy's output over and above what is required to keep the producers and their immediate families alive during the period of production. In a farming community, it would be whatever was left over from a crop after taking care of seed for the next year, and of minimal food rations for the farmers until the next crop. Economic surplus is difficult to measure precisely, since subsistence is difficult to define. In particular, people may be more productive, because they are stronger, if they get more food than is just needed to avoid starvation or diet-caused illness.

In any case, it is clear that all economies, except perhaps

the most primitive, are capable of producing an appreciable surplus, while in advanced economies the surplus represents by far the largest part of total output. Indeed, we shall have little need to talk in terms of the economic surplus in discussing rich and highly developed societies. But where the surplus is limited, it is useful to consider its size, its distribution, and its uses, bearing in mind the close relationships among these three aspects.

It is easiest to consider first the uses of surplus output. Such output can be used to improve the diet of producers, but they are likely to prefer exchanging at least a part of it for other goods; that is, they prefer to use it to feed non-farmers who build, weave, bake, or entertain for them. Part will also be stored, when possible, against the proverbial rainy day or dry spell. Some may go to members of the society whose productive economic role is at best indirect: medicine men, chiefs, priests, warriors, temple builders, poets, scholars, and idle noblemen. Indeed, we can summarize by stating that what we call civilization is made possible by the existence of an economic surplus. Finally, the surplus can be used to feed producers of a special category of goods and services which are not currently consumed by anyone but provide the possibility of increasing output later: tool and machine builders, teachers, land clearers, and builders of irrigation works, roads, barns, and vehicles. This process of reserving some surplus to ensure more output later is called *investment,* or the accumulation of capital. It is at the heart of the process of economic growth and will occupy us repeatedly.

Who gets the surplus will depend on the organization and institutions of the particular society, and we can indicate only how the distribution may affect the uses. If rich noblemen or powerful bishops own the land on which crops are grown, they will probably claim most of, if not all, the surplus, and the uses will reflect their tastes for finery, for impressive dwellings, and for the costly paraphernalia of war—or for good works and pious monuments. If the ruling power can tax producers heavily, a large share of the surplus may accrue to it, and again the uses can vary from building palaces and warships to supporting schools and building roads.

The size of the surplus depends to some extent on the bounty of nature, but its growth over time is closely tied to investment. Thus the surplus will be larger in the future if today's surplus goes to those who are willing to postpone its enjoyment and who depend on the productive power of new equipment to repay them amply for the delay. Who are these farsighted people? Again, there is no one answer. They may be thrifty peasants, expansion-minded businessmen, or a government concerned with the prospective welfare of its citizens or the future might of its armies.

We are thus left with dilemmas about the best uses of current surplus. Should it be used to enrich today's culture or to give everyone a slightly better life? Or should people be forced to postpone improvement in their own lot in order to secure a better future? This is a recurring problem, both for societies and for individuals, which can never find a once-and-for-all solution. But there is an even more agonizing dilemma—if the poor, who need it most, are given the surplus, they will eat it and there will be no investment; if the rich get it, they will probably save at least a part and make it available for investment, not because they are thrifty but because they have enough, so that postponing consumption, which will make them richer in the future, involves little present sacrifice. Yet it is only through investment that there can be any hope of increase in total output, without which the poor must remain poor. But this is largely a modern dilemma, and we must return to the dawn of European history and take up our survey.

CHAPTER 2

The Rise of
the Western Economy

Of the fifteen centuries since the fall of the Roman Empire, fully six were long relegated to historical limbo with the conveniently obscure tag of the Dark Ages. The standard story is quickly told: Rome fell, the barbarians finishing what moral decay had begun; then anarchic darkness fell over Europe; bands of Germanic warriors roamed the land, fighting one another when they were not defending themselves from even fiercer invaders; relative peace and a semblance of organization returned after the year 1000, perhaps because of general exhaustion.

What can we add to this unfairly flippant story, using our concept of an economic surplus? Really quite a lot, bearing in mind the little that has come down to us in the form of documents and other evidence. Medievalists are amazingly ingenious in building on frail and scattered traces of human activity, and so are great fun to read (despite their disturbing habit of assuming that you can read Latin, Old French, and German as easily as your newspaper).

Let us first look at Rome. The Roman Empire, whose grandeur has fascinated the West ever since the days of the Empire, would seem to have enjoyed a very large surplus indeed. In fact, its surplus was rather small, but it was very efficiently gathered from a wide area. Part was used to build the temples and circuses, the patrician houses and country villas that have since made the words Roman and ruin go together like ham and eggs. Part was used to support a large group of urban plebeians and to keep them out of mischief. When Caesar said, "Give them bread and circuses," he was being quite precise, for the plebeians were subsidized on both counts. But a large part of the surplus was reserved for the specific purpose of ensuring that it could be gathered regularly. It paid for tax collectors, for soldiers to keep the peace, and for roads to bring goods and travelers to Rome and other towns. Yet little was done to increase productivity, that is, the amount of surplus. Most food was grown by slave labor on large estates owned by absent patricians, or by the inhabitants of conquered lands, whose main contact with the Empire was through the tax collector.

An economic system so organized was a fragile thing. If the surplus declined for any reason, it became difficult to pay for the means of collecting it and then the decline became cumulative. The Empire could not cope with economic adversity; either it was great and powerful or it was doomed. Perhaps we must assign less of a role in its demise to the moral laxity of the times, and risk the accusation of economic determinism.

What of the barbarians, of whom we must remember that they owe their unflattering name to Latin writers? They first entered the Empire not as troublemakers but largely as soldiers and farmers. These were increasingly hard to recruit from the local population, and it seems the newcomers were rather better at farming, in particular, than the locals. Their plows could turn the heavy soils of the north better than the Roman implements. But apparently the barbarians were unwilling to give up their surplus to maintain imperial cities for which they had no taste, and so it became harder to keep the tenuous and far-flung Empire viable. As the Empire weakened, its hold over the non-Roman population loosened and the barbarians moved in to end its domination.

After the fall of Rome, Europe continued to live. This trite statement implies that economic activity also continued. In fact, enough was produced to keep the population from dying out, although it did decrease. A sufficient surplus remained to pay for the endemic warfare and even to provide chiefs and warriors with a few luxuries brought from the East. So trade did not disappear, nor, as we shall see, was it confined to a trickle of spices and rich fabrics. What happened was that a new aristocracy emerged, on the basis of the ability to fight and especially to maintain the horses and the expensive metal accoutrements required for warfare in post-Roman times.

How did the warriors gain control over the necessary economic surplus? Undoubtedly, might often made right, but outright requisitioning was not the only method used. The fighting man had something to offer the humble peasant; namely, protection from those who would have taken the surplus and the rest as well, and many men were willing to trade surplus and even a measure of freedom for such security. To be sure, the warrior himself could make the protection necessary for those who might have preferred independence. Thus, a new man was born, the serf—neither slave nor free. Instead of having been a former free peasant, the serf might also have been a former slave, for the decline of authority and stability made it difficult to run a purely servile economy. It was easier to grant the slave a piece of land and to require from him various services and payments, in other words to retain most of his surplus. But here let us make an explicit qualification. Throughout the period, indeed through most of the Middle Ages, Europe continued to know both free peasants and true slaves along with serfs.

Looking at Western Europe as a whole, we see only anarchy and violence. No ruler had effective authority over any sizable area, and the nobles fought one another or united only briefly to resist outside invaders. There were also outlaws who attacked villages and lay in wait for the rare trader who ventured to carry goods or other valuables. The brief unification of the land under Charlemagne around the year 800 A.D. was superficial, and in any case did not outlive him. Yet on the local level a viable social and economic order was forming, based on the authority of an armed noble and on the production of the serf peasants whom he controlled. This was the manor. It was, as it had to be, very nearly self-sufficient, using its surplus to provide the lord with a certain degree of rude comfort and the community as a whole with some protection against attack and famine.

Slowly, in the course of perhaps two centuries, some real measure of stability and peace was achieved in Europe. The Magyar invaders settled in Hungary, the Vikings in Normandy and England, while in Spain the Christians began five arduous centuries of "reconquest." Not until the famous year 1492 would they drive the last Saracens from the peninsula. The activity and influence of the Church contributed greatly to internal peace; the Church thus contributed more to economic activity than it could ever offset by all its moral strictures against trade and finance. Bishops kept alive towns that had little other reason for survival. Monasteries not only preserved literacy and literature, but also ran some of the largest and most efficient manors and kept techniques from dying out owing to war and unrest. Finally, the earliest extended cases of truce in relations between men were enforced not by rulers but by the Church. When the "Peace of God" was proclaimed for a certain time and region, it was observed even by robber barons and near-outlaws. As agricultural techniques were also progressing at the same time, a growing surplus could be mobilized for purposes other than war and defense. This set the stage for increased trade and greater wealth. Now that people had more to lose, there was even more reason to limit unpredictable and arbitrary violence.

It should not be thought that war, lawlessness, and danger were quickly or completely banished from Medieval Europe; indeed they probably increased again in the fourteenth century. But in an age when human life was cheaper than we like to think it is today, men clearly felt there was a good enough chance of success and survival to justify an impressive amount of enterprise, building, and accumulation.

CHAPTER 3

The Rural Economy
of Preindustrial
Europe

Agriculture changed slowly in preindustrial Europe. Newer techniques and patterns of organization only gradually displaced older and even highly inferior systems. Yet this very fact contributed to a bewildering variety of conditions that would plague us no matter how detailed our study of European agrarian life over some nine centuries.

No economic activity is really "just a job" to the people engaged in it, and preindustrial agriculture more than any other was—and is—a way of life. What makes it so is the primary concern for ownership and control of land. To the modern economist, land is a factor of production, that is, one of the ingredients, along with labor, skill, equipment, and knowledge for producing goods. In nonindustrial societies, however, land is that and much more. Security, status, wealth, and legitimate power are all closely tied to the possession of land. Rich and poor alike make great efforts to acquire it and to conserve what they have. This sometimes means obtaining clear ownership, but often involves securing various rights of tenure or payment for use. Unless the importance of land in such societies is realized, the history of European agriculture will just not make sense. And what is more, neither will current events, for in non-Western countries today, land tenure has more economic importance and political force than almost any other question. Land reform is what people really care about and will fight for, or resist, to the end, whether in Cuba or in Vietnam.

Turning back to the early Middle Ages, unsettled conditions and the absence of order through law meant that the warrior elite could control as much land as they found it profitable to hold. As we have seen, they either took it by the force or threat of arms, or acquired it in exchange for protection from the force of others. Only the Church based its power on moral authority, over clerics and laymen both, and this was sufficient to give monasteries control over large areas of land.

In this society, the basic unit of production was the manor, successor to the Roman estate or villa. Ideally, each manor had a lord, although one lord—cleric, nobleman, or king—might hold many manors. He, or his steward if the lord resided elsewhere, occupied the main building, which was also the fortress. Around this house were workshops, barns, and servants' quarters, while the cottages of the serfs were grouped nearby or perhaps formed a village some distance off. All sorts of activities we would classify today as industrial were carried on in this central part of the estate, from food processing to cloth weaving and leather tanning, for the manor was essentially self-sufficient. Yet farming remained the principal occupation, and land structure the most characteristic feature of the manorial system.[1]

A part of the land was reserved for the direct use of the lord; the rest served to maintain the serfs or was used for communal purposes. However, this was an abstract division. Physically, the distinctive subunits of the manor depended

---

[1] Many manors differed from the ideal type, and were simply agricultural communities owing payment to a lord who lived elsewhere.

on function rather than ownership. . . . The cultivated land was divided into two or three large fields, in addition to carefully tended and precious gardens and vineyards. Much of the area covered by the manor consisted of forest or uncultivated "common" or "waste." The arable fields were, of course, the heart of the enterprise, despite the importance of the forest for fuel, fodder, fruit, and as a game preserve. Every field was divided into long strips, each belonging either to the lord's domain or to a serf's holding. The land was not held in common, but it was frequently worked by teams of serfs pooling their equipment, animals, and muscles, especially for plowing and harvesting. This helped get the work done, but made it impossible for anyone to try different methods or crops, the more so as animals were allowed to graze in the fields as soon as the harvest was in.

Open fields with many owners were an important factor retarding improvement in agricultural techniques. Nevertheless, they were characteristic of the most productive regions of Europe, where deep plowing and three-field crop rotations were the general practice. In the cool, well-watered provinces near the Atlantic Ocean, peasants raised cattle and sheep on hedgerow-enclosed, individual pastures. And in the lands around the Mediterranean, although men gathered in large villages, they farmed small, irregular patches of dry and rocky soil. In contrast, fertile and irrigated southern valleys were rich with orchards and gardens.

Although property limits in forest and common could not be physically marked off as they could in the fields, the rights of lord and serf were carefully defined and vigorously contested. To a large extent, it was a permanent struggle between the peasants' need to cut wood and graze pigs and cattle and the lord's love of hunting. When and where the forest retreated as fields were carved out for a growing population, the conflict became sharp. There was also a larger struggle between the owners of great wandering flocks and herds and those who wished to farm and hunt in the country through which the animals passed on their seasonal migrations. Europe, like the American West, knew the rivalry between rancher and farmer, the age-old struggle of Abel with Cain.

It should not be thought that all of Europe, or even all of Western Europe, was organized in manors. There were independent peasants, isolated or in villages, and there were still estates worked by slaves. But by the eleventh century, virtually every European was either in the Church, a nobleman, or somehow dependent on a lord as his bondsman. And the clergy and nobles had their own hierarchies, the latter owing allegiance to their liege, or feudal lord. What interests us particularly is the system of payments that the combination of feudalism and manorialism imposed on those who tilled the soil and tended the animals.

From our distant and theoretical vantage point, we can summarize quite simply the relations between serf and lord, or peasant and noble. They were designed to transfer to the master at least a part of the surplus produced by the man. This surplus was used to finance a (relatively) more luxurious way of life, to pay for wars, and, particularly when the lord was a churchman, for charity, building, and the other activities of the Church. We would like to know how heavy the burden was, and in particular whether it left any surplus for the peasant, remembering also the need to retain some surplus to improve productivity. Clearly, the lord had the bulk of the power, except that in this unlettered age custom tempered its arbitrary use. Yet the institutional arrangements and the actual practice not only are poorly known, but were often so diverse and confused, that no good answer can be given. Let us try, however, to consider what we do know, and to show how the medieval hodgepodge of arrangements evolved into modern systems of land tenure and taxation.

A peasant had obligations to a lord either as his bondsman or because he held land from the lord. Frequently, the serf had to pay on both grounds, not always to the same lord. He owed a tenth of his income to the Church. And finally, whoever controlled the larger region, be he a great lord, a bishop, or a king, also had claims on his subjects. Obligations took the form of services, such as the duty to farm the lord's domain, and of payments in money or in kind. Payments especially were bewilderingly varied, ranging from death taxes to required use of the lord's mill. Indeed, any occasion, great or small, was sufficient excuse for some exaction or other. Finally, lords dispensed justice, considered less a means of social control than a source of revenue through fines. Most of the payments were small in themselves: a chicken, a measure of corn, a silver penny; but the poor peasant was never free of them, and he was lucky if two lords did not settle their arguments over who was owed what by both trying to collect.

With time, the burdens became, if not lighter, at least somewhat simpler. When nobles chose activity other than supervision of their own domain, and despaired of finding an honest steward to manage it for them, they "commuted" the services owed them into additional rent payments, and rented the domain to peasants eager for more land. Often, to be sure, the real value of rents declined as prices rose, and nobles had to compensate by finding new payments or increasing fines and taxes. Such attempts were among the causes of recurrent peasant wars. Yet the savage—and unsuccessful—uprisings of the fourteenth and fifteenth centuries are hard to explain on economic grounds; for example, they often occurred in regions and periods of relative prosperity, although there was always sufficient hardship and oppression to goad poor men to desperate revolt.

The personal obligations of bondsmen were gradually terminated in much of Europe when serfs purchased their freedom, individually or by communities. And in time the judicial and taxing functions were taken from local nobles by sovereign governments. But the legal distinctions between noble and commoner and between freeman and bondsman, so full of social vexation and arbitrary authority, were very slow to give way in Europe. They faded from the fifteenth to the seventeenth centuries in England, went out with a flourish in the French Revolution, but lingered until the mid-nineteenth century in parts of Germany and in Russia. Actually, many of the peasants of Eastern Europe had become serfs again at a relatively late date, when great landlords turned once again to cultivating their estates directly.

The pattern that emerged after the Middle Ages in Western Europe saw many peasants who owned their own land, and many others who rented their fields for cash or for a part of the crop. Holdings varied in size from tiny plots that would not feed a family, through prosperous family farms, to large holdings worked for profit, much like a factory. Often the tenant farmers were more prosperous than those who worked their own land, for a farsighted landlord would leave his farmer a good share of the surplus to invest in the enterprise.

Although the lord of the manor no longer hovered over any visible surplus, ambitious and debt-ridden governments now sent their tax collectors to peasant homes, and the prudent man still found it advisable to avoid showing signs of prosperity. The system was still far from just. The great landowners, Church and nobility, were still exempt from the bulk of taxes everywhere on the Continent. Only in England were chances more nearly equal, and it is no coincidence that most progress was made there, when agriculture took its great strides in the period of European growth unfairly called only the Industrial Revolution.

Gradual and hesitant, the changes in land tenure reflected slow and incomplete progress in farming methods. In discussing agricultural technology, we must drastically modify our usual notion of invention, followed by displacement of the old method by the new. A technique might be known and even practiced on a number of farms with clearly better results, yet two hundred years later the old method would persist a few miles away from the most dedicated partisans of the new. By way of partial explanation, we shall suggest a few reasons after making a brief survey of the main changes and continuing problems.

The technical change that took place in the early Middle Ages enabled men to farm larger areas of land, of which there was plenty. This was necessary, since the yield per acre was and remained very low. To understand the innovations, it is necessary only to look carefully at the classical picture of the farmer: a man walking behind an iron plow pulled by one or two horses. Three elements in this picture, though taken for granted today, together represented a great advance. One is the plow itself, long known, with its curved and sharp-edged share, which turned over the soil instead of merely scratching it. During the Middle Ages, wheels and a moldboard were added. Another is the material, iron, so much harder and more durable than wood. Although iron was known far back in ancient times, it was, for long, a rare and precious material and centuries passed before it was widely used on farms. Even then, most implements and early machines were of wood, with iron reserved for cutting edges and other critical, highly stressed parts. We think of iron as more abundant in medieval times because weapons were made of it, but, then as now, only the best would do for war. Peaceful pursuits, even those essential to survival, had to make do with lesser means.

Finally, there is the horse. For a long time the slow ox was preferred for heavy work, such as plowing. The horse was not considered strong enough, and no wonder. He had to drag the plow by a rope tied around his neck, and the harder he pulled, the less air found its way into his lungs. So the humble horse collar, resting the load on the animal's shoulders, made a tremendous difference. Those who like to collect revolutions in human history can add this one to their list, and pretty near the top at that.

As population increased in the Middle Ages, more land was needed, and the great forests of Europe gave way before the ax and the saw. Land had to be cleared not only because there were more mouths to feed, but also because soil wore out after years of cropping. Settlements spread out in Western Europe, while further east there was a real frontier, much like the American northern Midwest in the first half of the nineteenth century. But there were limits to the suitable land that could be plowed up without depriving lords of their hunting lands and graziers of their pastures. So other changes became necessary, to make more intensive use of existing acreage, and if possible, to retard soil exhaustion. Instead of the soil lying idle one year in two, many areas now grew crops two years out of three, which was possible if the crops were suitably chosen and if the land was prepared better. New crops, such as oats and legumes (beans, peas), were often sown between years of wheat or rye. Moreover, the growth of trade and industry made it possible to specialize each area in suitable crops or to grow special plants such as grapevines, flax, or dye-yielding woad and madder.

Nonetheless, the basic limitation of insufficient and declining soil fertility prevented decisive and steady progress. Steady population growth put pressure on the supply of food, while scarcity of food increased the virulence of epidemics and the impact of crop failures. In recent times, agriculture has come to depend heavily on direct addition of nutritive elements to the soil, and on the beneficial action of certain crops and improved mechanical working. But the first major step of the modern era was to join the two main branches of agriculture, arable farming and animal husbandry, thus improving them both. Until this was done, farmers were fighting a defensive battle against soil exhaustion.

What was the problem? In the Middle Ages, plowed land was almost exclusively reserved for growing crops to feed humans. Animals grazed on the stubble and on whatever natural pasture was available. As a consequence, there was insufficient fodder, especially in winter; furthermore, the fields were not well manured. Comparatively few animals could be kept, and many of these did not survive the winter.

The solution was to grow fodder so the animals would have sufficient pasture in summer and abundant hay in winter, and then to make full use of increased amounts of manure from field and stall, thus ensuring bigger crops and continued soil fertility.

The elements of the new farming were known by the end of the Middle Ages and were practiced on a limited number of farms, mainly large ones run for profit by men with an untraditional view of landowning. Why did new practices fail to spread? This question brings us to the larger question of the pace of technical change in preindustrial agriculture, and we might just as well admit that we still know relatively little about the dynamics of rural modernization. We can only suggest a few reasons. One was the system of open fields and forced rotation, which we have observed on the manor and which continued long after the medieval manor had become a legend. This imposed conformity on a whole group and made it impossible for an innovator to show his skeptical neighbors first and argue with them later. But technical conformity was a powerful force even when producers were not interdependent, as they were in the traditional farming system, and traditionalism was strong in handicrafts as well. In an age when few could read or write and when most men did not think of material things as obeying physical laws that could be learned through experiment and deduction, technology was in constant danger of deteriorating as skilled men grew old and died. Knowledge was handed down in stylized form, in which valuable techniques were inextricably combined with errors and irrelevant ritual. It was considered risky, if not downright immoral, to tinker with the mysteries entrusted to men by the past. The figure of the apprentice sorcerer, who could not control what he had set in motion, haunted the minds of men.

Finally, and perhaps most important, the margin for experiment and mistakes was terribly small. If a new method failed, the result was not merely a lack of improvement, but also loss of the crop and possible starvation. Our modern economy is based on the principle that a bird in the hand should cheerfully be sacrificed for one and one-quarter birds in the bush, but we have confidence in our ability to guess right often enough, and are also rich enough to finance the mistakes that are the price of trying something new.

Europe had to wait until attitudes loosened enough to let new men emerge, men who would resist the weight of tradition and accept the risk of social opprobrium as well as economic ruin. A new kind of adventurer was needed, one for whom the satisfaction of accomplishment and the prospect of great material rewards mattered more than security or the approval of his neighbors.

CHAPTER 4

Trade and
Urban Life in the
Middle Ages

We are justified in speaking of the manor as being very nearly self-sufficient. Nonetheless, throughout the first centuries after the fall of the Roman Empire in the West, a trickle of trade continued to flow into and over Europe. In view of the conditions prevailing—the absence of security and of facilities for commerce—even this trickle is eloquent witness to the tremendous economic gains that exchange can bring. A sizable additional surplus could be generated when local produce was swapped for goods that could not be produced locally, such as salt, steel weapons, fine fabrics, glass, furs, or dried fish. What if transport trebled the price? The salt that one man could gather on the shores of the Baltic in a day fetched many man-days worth of grain on the banks of the Seine, so there was room to pay transport costs and to cover the risk of loss as well.

Some settlements specialized early, not so much because they found good opportunities for acquiring other goods on better terms than they could produce them at home, but out of dire necessity. The most active traders of northern Europe were the Frisians, who presumably had found refuge from warlike enemies in the sandy dunes along the North Sea. They could fish, dry salt, and later weave cloth, but required trade to supply them with grain and lumber.

For them and for others, specialization, which implied trade, meant more effective use of resources, since few areas are well suited for the variety of production needed to meet all the needs of even a primitive economy. In addition, specialization created its own justification. By growing or making a product, people acquired a skill that commanded a good price. When techniques are primitive, there is a considerable premium for quality goods, and the lord of a self-sufficient manor was only too glad when he could stop trying to make do with what his crude workshops could turn out or his recalcitrant soil put forth.

European trade in early medieval times consisted of two basic types. One was a vestige of the Mediterranean trade that had flourished under the Romans and now brought a few luxuries to the clergy and the nobility. The imports consisted of silk and "spices," the latter a generic name for any precious substance, from dyes and drugs to the pepper and cloves used to season and preserve food (or disguise its dubious freshness). Barbarian Europe was actually an outpost of this trade, a backwater for the center at Byzantium, where the Eastern Empire carried on with diminished power. So small a trade required little paraphernalia in the way of towns, professional merchants, or financial arrangements, and we therefore have little written record of it. The counterflow from Europe consisted of lumber and iron and of slaves, this last a trade that slowly faded, because Europe neither found them useful nor was willing to sell Christians into slavery. Moral considerations did not, however, hinder revival of the slave trade when the Europeans began to exploit colonial plantations.

The other kind of trade, though it is even more anonymous, was almost certainly more extensive. It involved the movement of staples in addition to a few native luxuries such as furs and amber, over short as well as longer distances. All kinds of food products seem to have traveled, from vegetables bound for a village or for one of the rare towns, to casks of wine and bags of wheat carried from one manor to another belonging to the same lord. Even less than in the case of luxuries from the East did this trade involve professionals or give rise to institutional traces or systematic records. Yet we have enough incidental and indirect references to it to be confident of its reality.

The invaders who prolonged anarchy and violence by their attacks in the tenth century turned out in the end to be helpful for European commercial activity. Although the Saracens were, by taste, landsmen rather than sailors and had an ideological quarrel with the Christians, they represented an advanced and highly commercial society. Despite piracy and holy war, it seems that the Mediterranean carried more goods to and from Europe after the Moslem conquest than before. Historians used to be impressed by the incompatibility of ideological conflict and commercial relations, but we have the experience of the Cold War to teach us that the two can perfectly well coexist, even in an age, such as ours, that prides itself on rationality and consistency.

The Vikings who swooped down out of Scandinavia were, on the other hand, superb sailors and intrepid navigators, as evidenced by their voyages to Greenland and North America. At first content to plunder and destroy, they were soon permanently attracted to the green fields of Normandy and England, and remained to conquer and settle. They took over and greatly expanded northern trade, even sailing and portaging their ships on the great rivers of Russia to the Black Sea to trade. In the Baltic and North seas, they carried fish and salt, wool and honey, grain and furs. They made possible the first truly "modern" specialization: a cloth industry in Flanders supplied with wool from the rural outpost of England.

To the south, trade was also reviving, and another people

of the low-lying coasts, like the Frisians, took the lead. The fishermen and salt gatherers of Venice, nominally ruled by the hard-pressed Byzantine Empire, built a trading power that soon overshadowed the capital at Constantinople, and for centuries controlled much of the rich Mediterranean trade. Indeed, Italy had never completely lost its urban character and its ties to the East, and the revived trade remained different from what emerged farther north. The cities were in complete charge, and the business of the cities was business. Even the nobles, who in the North left commerce and even the management of their estates to others, were in Italy also the greatest merchants or backers of merchants.

In time, however, Venice had to share trade with other cities. Genoa occupied a similar position on the other flank of northern Italy, and the two were perennial rivals. But even cities not on the sea, foremost among them Florence, became great trading powers. To compensate for their distance from the sea, the Florentines developed prosperous silk and wool industries.

Although we have long since abandoned the idea that Europe knew nothing of the East and its goods before the Crusaders returned with dazzled eyes to their rude huts and fortresses, the wars against the Moslems did have a considerable economic impact. The great beneficiaries were the Italians. Not only could they improve their trading position in the Near East behind the military successes of Christian warriors, but they were well, if not always promptly, paid for carrying the soldiers and furnishing them with supplies. Nor should we neglect the increase in demand for Eastern goods when veterans returned and began to spin tales in the alehouses and banquet halls.

The accomplishments of the Italian city-states, despite their small size, are one of the great wonders of the times. We are familiar with the wealth of artistic and architectural masterpieces they have left. But when viewing the stones and canals, and in recapturing the adventures of the Uffizis and the Estes, it is easy to forget that they were, in reality, sidelines to the main business of the towns: commerce, shipping, and industry.[2]

In the North too, the revival of long-distance trade went hand in hand with the growth, almost the rebirth there, of towns. Merchants needed a place to store goods, to shelter themselves on the journey and through the winter, and to carry out their buying and selling. Such places had to be safe, of course, but they also had to afford a freedom of enterprise that was missing in the feudal pattern of law and custom. Originally, a merchant, not being noble, was a serf. He could not come and go as he pleased, could not trade except by his lord's leave, and normally had to pay over some portion of everything he carried. So towns could be centers of commerce only if they became islands of privilege from manorial exactions. The necessary privileges were acquired from the lords, often bishops, by purchase or struggle. The legend of towns as early small democracies has been greatly overdrawn, but to be a burgher, a citizen of a "free city," was to know a breadth of opportunity unparalleled in medieval times.

During the most flowering years of the Middle Ages, from perhaps 1000 to 1300, trade prospered and grew. As goods became more available, rural lords began to specialize production more and to sell in the market. Or else they demanded payment of taxes and rents in coin, leaving it to the peasants to market their own crops. But though the supply of goods and money increased, the nobles' hunger for new goods and for cash to finance a new scale of life was never satiated. Luxuries, wars, crusades, tourneys, all these absorbed anything the estates could produce and a bit over, so that it was often necessary to demean oneself and deal with the money lender or with a merchant from the city. In the

2 If one reads the history of a city such as Florence, it hardly seems possible that fighting and international politicking left any time for either art or business, especially since the last phase of every civil war in Florence was the burning down, by the winners, of the proud towers of the losers.

end, these same merchants would buy or take over land, and in a generation or two be landed aristocrats themselves.

Let us look briefly at trade in this heyday. The two centers were northern and central Italy on the one hand and Flanders on the other. Bruges was the Venice of the North in more than just her canals. London, Cologne, Arras were her outposts. From both major centers trade flowed out across the sea and in through the rivers and lanes of the Continent. The two currents met on the plains of Champagne, in eastern France, where a series of fairs allowed merchants to meet. Fairs were important so long as supplies and markets were not secure all over Europe. But they also provided a place for financial transactions, not least the conversion of coins.

We must pause to say a word about the business of coinage, another of these awkward subjects too complex to sort out and too important to omit. The elegant Roman system of coins based on gold persisted in name for many years after the fall of the Empire, but the coins themselves hardly circulated. If Europeans by some chance had to deal in large sums of money, they used Byzantine or Arabic pieces. For the value of coins, especially large ones, is closely tied to the authority of the one who issues them and, presumably, guarantees their weight and composition.

Charlemagne, in his attempt to institutionalize the new rural order, emitted small silver pieces, appropriate to the modest trading needs of his day. These were pennies, and they were the smallest units in a monetary system, based on silver, which has survived to this day: the familiar £, s, d, (Libra, sol, denarus), or pound, shilling, and penny.

But Charlemagne could not prevent all sorts of authorities from minting their own coins, and the number of coins grew with time, gold pieces being added to silver. The task of figuring out equivalencies in the various currencies was nearly impossible. Not only were there many coins, with no simple ratios of value, but seemingly identical coins differed in fineness and weight or were clipped or counterfeited. The worst offenders were the issuers themselves, who could not

resist the temptation to make their stock of metal go a bit
farther by alloying it or by reducing the weight of coins.
Only with the powerful sovereign nation did the muddle
come to an end, and throughout European history the prestige and fortunes of a country could be read by the stability
of its money, not so much in terms of purchasing power as
in terms of metal content.³

But let us turn back to the animation and bustle of a
Champagne fair in the thirteenth century. The men who
specialized in the complex business of changing coins also
found themselves dealing in pieces of paper that, while not
money, acquired value from the pledges of reputable merchants to exchange them for money. Thus was born the bill
of exchange, though probably not precisely in Champagne;
with its extension, and with that of other financial instruments, the fairs were in fact doomed. Now merchants could
deal at a distance, letting their goods and signature travel
while they stayed at home.

Though their profession was now less adventurous, it still
remained risky, and the greatest merchants began to play an
especially perilous game. In addition to dealing in mer-
chandise and in other financial affairs (so much like the
loans at interest frowned on by the Church that only a *very*
sophisticated man could keep the two distinct), they began
to lend money to princes. Now the stakes were high but so
were the risks, for the prince could be defeated in battle,
forget the financier's services, or find an excuse to get rid of
him. The worst was that only by continuing to support a
monarch in trouble could the banker ever hope to recover
what he had already lent.

With the extension of their range of activity, merchants
also had to improve their business techniques. The Italians,

³ Habits acquired over centuries die hard, and even today many people attach great importance to the relation between metal and money,
whether they be French finance ministers or American conservatives. Yet
today, the backing for currency is not metal, even if the system retains
the use of gold. It is rather the will of a society, through its government,
to keep the banking system liquid, the price level free of sharp trends,
and the economy on an even keel.

masters of the commercial arts, invented double-entry book-keeping, but even with its help many great houses fell, victims of bad speculations, political disgrace, or the lures of a patrician existence.

If the merchant did not become a banker and hobnob with kings, he could still occupy his time when business no longer required him to ride over the map of Europe. Industry, particularly the major woolen and silk businesses, was dominated by merchants who coordinated the activity of many workshops along the path from raw material to valuable cloth. This reflected the importance of coordination, and of capital to finance the interval between buying the wool, say, and selling the cloth. By contrast, most of the equipment was cheap, and might be owned by poor workmen. The mining industry, on the other hand, tended to be under the direct control of rulers or great financiers.

Perhaps the reader will have wondered, in reading the descriptions of merchants and bankers, why we are neglecting the supposed cornerstone of medieval urban society, the independent craftsman. It is not our intention to slight the small masters who combined in a guild to protect and regulate their trade. They promoted social and technical stability by training apprentices and journeymen, and the guild insured that inferior work and dishonest practice would not hurt the reputation of the whole group.

Yet the craft guilds were neither so democratic nor so influential in urban government as they have commonly been portrayed. On the one hand, they were largely concerned with preserving themselves from competition by outsiders, such as rural artisans in the same region, and with limiting the number of masters by admitting chiefly the sons of masters to membership in the guild. Thus, in crafts as well as in early industry, many remained journeymen—or workers—through life, and never acceded to independence. On the other hand, there were sharp distinctions among masters and between guilds. While the cobbler or tailor, with three or four helpers, was socially little higher than his workers, the great clothiers and merchants, together with the urban

nobility, formed an urban patriciate that completely controlled the town. When one man employed many "journeymen," the whole business was indistinguishable from the
later relationship of factory owner and wage earner, except
that the state of medieval workers was worse than in industrial times. They usually had to furnish tools and their own
house, while their occasional attempts to organize or strike
were repressed with savagery.   1473992

In addition, the entrepreneurs fought the danger of increasing wages by taking their materials to less demanding
peasants outside the walls of the town. The textile industry
moved out of town, joining the heavy mining and smelting
industries. For some three hundred years, towns would have
mainly an administrative and commercial function. Only
with the advent of factories would there again be a close
connection between major industry and urban habitation,
but then the town would grow up around the factories,
rather than industry seeking labor in the towns. In the
twentieth century we have come full circle. Light and clean
manufacturing industries now follow people out to the
smaller towns and suburbs.

The social rigidity of which we have been speaking was a
product of the later Middle Ages, of the period when population declined from famine and plagues, and troubles and
wars increased. One of many historians' quarrels concerns
the question of whether trade also declined. We may just
say that it must at least have stopped growing, since all the
symptoms of crisis were present.

Let us pause a minute, and consider these symptoms.
From a certain point of view things seem to have gone much
better. More monuments were being built, informal groupings and agreements were being codified, more records were
being kept, and men increased their efforts to win and keep
markets. Yet on careful thought, all these things were signs
of difficulty rather than of greater opportunity. The Hanse,
the league of German trading cities that dominated Baltic
trade from the thirteenth century on, found it necessary to
formalize their union when the English, Danes, and Dutch

challenged their position. Hard-pressed kings gave honors and prestige to the bankers from whom they wanted more loans. Guild masters faced with poor business conditions hardened their resistance to competition and dignified their exclusiveness with more elaborate ritual. Despite the absence of reliable demographic statistics, often of anything that can be called statistics at all, historians are forced to conclude that population decreased sharply and that demand for goods fell with it, so times were hard. Endemic war, with its increased pressure on the part of tax collectors and with greater danger of violence and confiscation, did not alleviate the lot of merchants.

As usual, however, the loss of some was the gain of others. France, involved for over a century in intermittent war, suffered most. Southern Germany took over some of the North-South trade, while Catalonia and Antwerp enjoyed great prosperity. In general, those who supplied armies or dealt in the materials and articles of war could get rich, though keeping their wealth might prove another problem. Finally, England had emerged from her relatively humble economic role as a supplier of wool to Flanders, and was making her own cloth. As yet it had to be sent to Holland or Flanders to be finished, for the enterprising British would not be giving lessons of technology to the world for another three centuries. But, whether men knew it or not, the great days of the interior and of the "European" seas, Baltic, Mediterranean, Adriatic, were numbered. The following centuries—how many?—would belong to those with their eyes turned to the oceans.

Through conflicts and crises, it is easy to forget the tremendous and permanent changes that had taken place in Europe between the end of foreign invasions and the beginning of the sixteenth century. Economic life was marked by a large and almost irreversible increase of economic interdependence and specialization. More and more agricultural production found its way at least to local markets, while town dwellers and many farmers depended on nearby or distant workshops for a variety of processed goods, from flour and beer to tools and cloth. Numerous towns, almost always small by modern standards, subsisted largely on the commerce and industry generated by this exchange, while the concentration of people in turn provided a market for commercial production in the countryside. Finally, although Europe did not yet consist of a group of nations in the modern sense of the term, the sovereign authority of powerful rulers dominated most of its area. The system of multiple and competing authorities characteristic of the Middle Ages was giving way to centralized control and taxation. The process had gone farthest in the westernmost countries, the same group that in the next centuries derived added strength from their Atlantic orientation.

It would nonetheless be another 250 years before even the first European nation achieved the beginnings of true modern economic growth. What was there in the Europe of 1500 that held back the kind of sustained progress we associate with a modern economy? One important barrier, as we have already suggested, lay in the impossibility of achieving a permanent and substantial increase of the food supply relative to the population. Whenever food production rose, as when new land was cleared or better methods introduced, people found it possible to marry earlier, thus increasing the number of children. This factor in time limited the surplus that could be generated and put to the task of modernizing the economy. Sometimes, the temporary opportunity came not from an increase in the supply of food, but from a drop in population, as a result of plague or other causes. But each time the population rose again, encouraged by the very factors that resulted from the previous decline: more available land and a relatively hardy surviving population.

Another great difference between the economy of 1500 and that of 1800 relates the effects of trade on the economy of a region. As we have seen, there were changes in the flow of trade, and boom regions became backwaters as other towns and areas took over leadership. The remarkable fact was that such a boom left few economic traces of its passage. Some great centers of medieval activity did not recover for hundreds of years, and the magnificence of the past, expressed in stones, makes a striking contrast with the prolonged economic doldrums in which the great buildings have slept for so long. Preindustrial towns were like mining camps: when the one or two major activities declined, there was often nothing to take their place. By contrast, and looking ahead for a moment, later booms would trigger a whole series of expansions in related activities, so that growth would proceed even if the initial stimulus lost its force.

We can follow this phenomenon by looking for a moment at the diverse fortunes of European cities after the end of the Middle Ages. Those which emerged as the largest had indeed existed and been active for a long time, but seldom were they the leaders in medieval times. London, Paris, Milan, Naples, and Brussels were more active in the sixteenth and seventeeth centuries than were Florence, Venice, and Cologne. They combined commercial activity with new roles as centers of administrative, intellectual, and political life. Besides these, a new generation of cities emerged with the advent of the powerful sovereign, almost exclusively governmental in their nature. Such were Berlin and Madrid, while Rome and Vienna had meager economic activity for their size and stature.

To be sure, many commercial centers continued to prosper through all the changes in economic patterns, usually because of their geographic location as harbors or crossroads, or because they were particularly free of annoying restrictions to economic activity. These included Lyons and Marseilles, Frankfurt and Hamburg, Genoa and Geneva, and the queen of them all, Amsterdam. On the Atlantic coast, the shift in trade and power was reflected in the rise of busy ports, from Cadiz and Lisbon in the south, to Bordeaux and Nantes in France, and Bristol and Liverpool in the British Isles. Much later, an entirely different kind of urban entity would spring up: ugly, sprawling, planless, yet teeming with vitality in its mixture of wealth and squalor.

This was the industrial city, more often the industrial complex or region, such as the Midlands and Lancashire, the Ruhr, and the area around Lille.

The people of nineteenth-century Europe may be forgiven if they had doubts about the Industrial Revolution. How could one speak of progress to someone who compared Roubaix with Bordeaux, Manchester with Bristol, and Essen with Cologne? Indeed, our modern industrial society, with its untold power to produce wealth and material comforts, has never really come to terms with the city. Not that preindustrial cities can be judged fairly by their stately avenues and monuments, their picturesque and character-laden winding streets. They were killers too, where epidemics spread along open sewers and fire flashed through wooden houses, and every vice and crime flourished amid the city-dweller's conditioned indifference to his too-close neighbors. Yet, can we truly speak of progress when our present reaction to urban problems is to drown them in oceans and jungles of concrete? We shall speak of great achievements and progress in the next chapters, but it is well to remember that our unfinished economic business includes the need to reconcile efficiency and the human element in our cities.

Finally, European society still accorded relatively little importance to economic activity and withheld status from the commercial, industrial, and financial leaders who were required to manage the modernization of the economy. As we have suggested, they, and the men who allowed technology to break out of its limitations, were content to leave rank and privilege to representatives of the old order, at least for a long time. But they required at least freedom from the restrictions imposed on their ventures by religious, cultural, and political values.

We shall consider later the attitudes and institutions that grew up with the industrial economy, but first we shall examine the phenomenon of the market and shall follow European trade as it bursts out of its geographic bounds.

CHAPTER 5

The

Market Economy

Two fundamental and closely linked changes marked the transition of the European economy from medieval times to the industrial age. One was the tremendous improvement in productivity made possible, among other things, by the increased use of metals and new forms of energy. The other was the extension and freeing of economic exchange, leading to the formation of what is called a market economy. Western economists have been fascinated by markets, by the elegance and efficiency with which they guide the allocation of resources. But at the same time, their power to upset and shape society has led many to denounce and resist the free play of an exchange economy. Let us look briefly at markets, at their much-vaunted efficiency, and also at the reasons that have impelled men to interfere with them.

The need for exchange is part and parcel of the process of specialization and large-scale production behind any productive economy, even the simplest. To produce goods cheaply requires practice and specialized skill, as well as tools and concentration on a limited task. Specialization in production is reconciled with diversity in consumption by means of exchange. But exchange implies a rate: the quantity of one good equivalent to a given quantity of another; and the function of the market is to establish the "right" ratio, or the "right" price if we think of goods exchanging through the intermediary of money. What is the right price? It is the price that reflects the real scarcity of a particular good relative to others, taking into account *both* the resources necessary to produce it *and* the desire of consumers for the good.

Markets perform their function of allocating the scarce resources of a society because they act on both ends of the process, namely production and use. A high price, for example, encourages new sellers at the same time as it discourages buyers, so the "shortage" that brought about the high price is attacked from both sides. The market thus permits far-reaching specialization without a complex apparatus for coordinating decisions and without sacrificing the range of choice open to consumers and producers. The result has been greater surplus and economic growth, while the freedom to make economic decisions has given innovators a chance and has rewarded them when their initiatives, in fact, improved productivity or filled needs better.

Complications arise, however, because markets determine more than the rate of exchange between various goods, or between services and commodities. They also fix quantities that have a direct impact on the lives of human beings and communities. Incomes depend on the price of a good; occupations must be changed when the wages for a particular form of labor go down; families must move if the market offers them more income elsewhere; traditional patterns of consumption have to be modified as relative prices change. All this is the work of the impersonal market, simply of variations in prices and factor incomes, and it gives no rest. Not only can the changes bring great hardship, but the very fact of unpredictable and frequent change also strains the social fabric.

The market is no respecter of persons or of tradition, and is deaf to claims of justice, fairness, and stability. Yet it must be added that its harshness is at least nondiscriminatory, except insofar as the deprived are deprived also of the means to improve their future. Negro money is as good as white to the market, Republican as Democratic, and ham from Communist hogs will command the same price, if it tastes as good, as the Virginia or Iowa product. We should remember that the most usual alternatives to "charging what the traffic will bear" are paternalism or discrimination, not fairness and compassion.

Why, then, have markets been so persistently criticized in the abstract and interfered with in practice? There are a number of reasons, all of which will recur in our story as important factors in analyzing economic change. Here, we can do no more than mention some of them, with the reminder that it is not the economist's job to approve or condemn. He can only point out the costs of interference and also draw the historical lesson that it has proved harder to channel or thwart the market than one might think. Indeed, the social values behind such attempts may well bend to the needs of the market, in the end.

One class of induced market "imperfections" arises because higher prices mean higher incomes for sellers. If the goods or the labor that I have are scarce, my income will be correspondingly higher, and it therefore pays me to contrive a greater scarcity than exists. I can do this by keeping other sellers away from the buyers, that is, by creating a monopoly. The consequences are to restrict the volume of exchange, and therefore limit specialization, and also to send false signals ("artificial" prices) to all producers and consumers, thus distorting the allocation of resources. Note that these distortions, in addition to the transfer of income toward me, are a result of the artificially induced scarcity of my product or services.

Groups of people may also interfere with markets in order to preserve themselves from rapid social change. Historically, this has certainly occurred, but there has also been a countervailing change in the very values of the society, tending to make acceptable the qualities of fluidity and openness, or disregard for tradition, that allow the market to perform its ceaseless remolding of economic structures.

By far the most prevalent means of interfering with markets has been political action. Sometimes the state has acted at the behest of those who favored social stability or claimed the advantages of monopoly. Often the purpose has been to shift income away from those who were rewarded by the market and toward others whose claims were based on need, status, or power. But the state is also a claimant on the output of the economy, either in return for protective and organizational services or simply as an end in itself. The claims of the state on the society have been particularly important in the era of absolutism, as we shall see in the next chapter, and under modern fascist regimes. The role of government in furthering social and economic goals of the society it serves is a central aspect of current (and earlier) debates over economic growth. Finally, in socialist economies the state largely supersedes the market as the allocator of resources, determining in large part the structure of production, consumption, and incomes.

The market has also been attacked because it is closely tied with private ownership of the means of production. While it is not necessarily true that an exchange economy requires private property as the dominant form of organization for economic assets, both advocates and critics of the market economy have assumed that the two go together. We shall later have to evaluate socialism, the main alternative so far tried, and also the various attempts to compromise between a collectivized and commanded economy on the one hand, and a market with private ownership on the other.

CHAPTER 6

The Maritime
Expansion of Europe
from 1500 to 1750

The period prosaically referred to by historians as "early modern" was as turbulent and rich as any. During this period Western Europe really came into its own and began to assert a domination over the whole world that it has relinquished to its offspring and imitators only in this century. We shall first review briefly the general picture of economic life in Europe, and then focus on our most frankly glamorous episode, that of colonial expansion and mercantile trade.

It is tempting to sum up the period by saying that Europe was too busy to devote its best efforts to internal economic development. On the one hand, its peoples were working out the system of sovereign nations with central governments, and a troublesome one it was, becoming workable only when it was about to be submerged by international economic ties and revolutionary tides. On the other hand, individual energies were absorbed by great currents of intellectual and artistic activity. The Renaissance and the Enlightenment are only the most massive landmarks of this period, which saw the development of modern science, language, music, and much of our intellectual patrimony. Both these currents, the political and the intellectual, involved violent as well as peaceful activity, and it is often hard to disentangle dynastic or colonial wars from religious struggles.

In Germany and Italy particularly, one can say that economic life was marking time, slow progress in techniques barely compensating the destructions of war and the exhaustion of the soil. France and Spain did much more, but their economies were not geared to the heady ambitions of their rulers, and consequently fiscal pressure was often so sharp that it further hurt the economy.

The most intense economic activity took place in the Protestant countries, Holland and England. Yet even there, two centuries of effort did not produce sustained economic growth in the modern sense. Why? Were techniques of production not good enough to make a real breakthrough? Or did it require a long and slow gathering of momentum until the market became large enough to sustain truly productive methods requiring intense specialization? Adam Smith, writing just after the beginning of the era of modern growth, chose the latter explanation. In words that are the motto of economics, he proclaimed that *"The division of labor is limited by the extent of the market."* We shall not presume to argue with him, but only suggest timidly that it also works the other way.

So we can quickly pass over the limited changes that did take place: an industrial prerevolution in England in the sixteenth century, when coal replaced wood in many industrial processes (but not iron smelting!); the creation of royal manufactures in France; further development of banks and banking techniques; some enclosure of agricultural land in England, freeing farmers from the constraint imposed by open fields. There are many more changes, but they are important chiefly as early signs of what was to come, and are best considered as the precursors of industrialization. At the time, their effects in even the most prosperous countries were limited.

Instead, we shall turn to the greatest economic adventure of European history, the maritime expansion of European power and trade. This occupied the imaginations of contemporaries as well as the energies of policy makers, and the story loses nothing in being told from an economic point of view.

The expansion of Europe is so familiar a part of the history of Atlantic man that its astounding character is often forgotten. Not only was it accomplished with ludicrously small forces, primitively equipped, but its start came at a particularly inauspicious time for Europe. In the fifteenth century, the feud between European Christians and the tri-continental power of Islam was going poorly for the Western side. Although there was still much talk of crusade, Europe was on the defensive. In fact, it had been on the defensive for some time, except in Spain, where the reconquest was slowly but steadily pursued. But our view of the medieval Crusades suffers from the usual cheering-section approach to history, particularly as taught in schools. The successes of the European crusaders were largely limited to a short period during which the Moslems were more divided than they. Most of the time it was the other way around, and the counter-Crusade made headway. The Moslems also had the advantage of a disciplined and fast cavalry against the glamorous, but clumsy and individualistic, armed knight. Finally, the rising Moslem group was the Turks, who had no peers in fighting. So defeat followed defeat for the Christians, with the fall of Constantinople in 1453 a gloomy portent of possible attacks on Europe itself.

How then did the tide turn so decisively? An economic historian, Carlo Cipolla, has suggested that the development of the gunned sailing ship by the Europeans was the prime factor. In this case, the spirit of inquiry and experiment, rather than religious zeal, was the driving force that turned back the power of Islam. Nor should we forget the lure of wealth. Whatever the motives, trade and conquest went hand in hand, and it would have been unthinkable for the hard-pressed European powers to continue financing and manning expeditions if their only goals had been the propagation of faith and flag.

As anyone knows, the Europeans were primarily interested in spices, by which it is clear that we mean not only the vital preservers and seasoners of food, but any valuable article that came from the East. It has long been thought that the growing power of the Turks endangered or cut off the flow of spices from Asia. This is not true, but Turkish power did make spices more expensive. To understand the problem, and the whole mercantile approach to trade, it is necessary to look a bit more closely at the market for spices. Compared to the potential quantity Europe could use, and also to the potential for production in the Far East, the amount that actually flowed was very small. Thus it was possible to have a very low price for spices at the production end and a very high one in Europe. This situation in turn made the trade itself highly lucrative, so the Europeans were far more interested in capturing the spice trade than in just getting spices. And this is the fundamental motive of all the national policies and strategies of foreign trade in the mercantile period: not to gain from the specialization that active trade would allow, but to capture the profits from limited trade in products with a high margin between production cost and final selling price. But it must be emphasized that this strategy required two precautions: first, obviously, to prohibit anyone else, such as foreigners, from competing; second, to limit the amount of trade, for fear of diminishing the spread between buying and selling price.

But we must return for a moment to the story of techniques, although it is not strictly an economic one, and summarize the story of the gunned sailing ship, the vehicle of European triumph. Neither firearms nor, of course, the sailing ship was new in 1450, but the standard weapons were still the armed cavalry on land and the rowed galley on the

Mediterranean. Cannon existed, but they were expensive, not very good, and, above all, suffered from the same transport problems plaguing overland commerce. It was not until the seventeenth century that cannon were much used on land except to attack or defend fixed fortifications. But just as water transport was much more efficient for goods, it soon also became a good carrier of firepower.

The requirements of carrying cannon and of sailing oceans instead of inland seas led to a great change in the design of ships. By stages, square sails replaced triangular ones, oars disappeared, and more masts were added. By 1500, the basic ideas were known, but there was considerable development for the next century or so. The early trend was to make both guns and ships bigger and bigger, whereas maneuverability, speed, and cost were more sophisticated goals and therefore developed more gradually. We can mention only two great advances in ship design: the piercing of portholes, which allowed the cannon to be placed low in the waist; and, later, the specialization of ships by function, warships being distinguished from merchantmen. This last helped the upstart English and Dutch to compete with the dominant Spaniards, who did not separate the two kinds of vessel.

It still remains for us to consider why the gunned sailing ship should have proved so decisive, and also why the Europeans conserved for so long their advantage in transportation and firepower. First of all, they took full advantage of their superior weapons and of the disunity among the local populations. Except in South and Central America, the Europeans stuck for a long time to coastal enclaves, which could be defended from the sea, while their strategy took advantage of the existence of earlier oppressors or occupying powers. These could either be displaced, as in Mexico and Peru; used, as in securing slaves on the African coast; or fought with the cooperation of the population, as in south India.

The other question, why the Moslems in particular refused to change their means of warfare, transport, and production, is far more speculative. Perhaps they were aware of the tremendous upheavals in every facet of life that would inevitably follow once the search for improvement became the prime force guiding economic activity. Professor Cipolla sees a conscious decision not to pay the cultural price of economic growth, and there is certainly evidence of this for Japan. Whatever the reason, an irresistible wave of imperialism spread out through the Atlantic and Indian oceans, and by 1700 the Europeans controlled every current of trade touching Europe, as well as the slave trade from Africa to the West Indies and some flows of gold and ivory from West Africa to the East.

Let us look for a moment at the chronology of expansion and at the role of the different Atlantic powers. The first power was clearly the Portuguese, who were so busy and so successful in developing the route to Asia around Africa that they felt it a waste of resources to encourage the fuzzy geographical ideas of a Genoese adventurer who thought Asia was within striking distance to the west. Nor were they wrong, since by 1500 they were busy hauling spices from India, whereas Columbus never came within 10,000 miles of Asia! But his chance discovery did get the Spaniards into the race, and they eventually found metals, if not spices, as well as docile natives for the service of mine owners. Eventually, however, the new lands to the west did not furnish enough labor for the sugar fields that rivaled the mines in value, and Africa had to be tapped.

By 1550, the famous Treaty of Tordesillas, signed in 1494 between Spain and Portugal, seemed a reasonable agreement between the two powers effectively engaged in colonization and exploration outside Europe. It was not really until the seventeenth century that it stood out as a monument of presumption on the part of two nations trying to divide the world, with Papal blessing. Until that time, the other powers with mercantile aspirations had to make do with the crumbs from the Iberian feast. Their ships competed with the Portuguese in developing the Newfoundland fisheries, preyed on Spanish commerce in the Caribbean, and tried to capture some of the trade furnishing slaves and supplies to the Spanish colonies, despite the strict prohibition on such activity by foreigners.

It was Holland which first made serious breaches in the Spanish and Portuguese trading empires. In the East, the newly independent Dutch showed great ability in the difficult task of controlling the spice trade in the face of overwhelming opposition by local rulers and Moslem traders. The Dutch replaced the faltering Portuguese, relying on better organization and direct control over the spice islands themselves, rather than on Indian bases. The full magnitude of their achievement, aside from the suffering and oppression inflicted on the inhabitants, can only be appreciated if one takes into account the size of Holland and the fact that the Dutch were dealing with far more advanced societies than the Spaniards were in America.

In the West, the Dutch took advantage of a fundamental contradiction in the organization of the Spanish Empire. This grandiose undertaking was based on a backward home economy, which was doing nothing to emerge from this stagnation. Agriculture suffered from the domination of the sheep interests, which maintained the right to graze their immense flocks across Castille, eroding land and limiting the growing of crops. Modern enterprise was stifled by tax pressures and by an archaic social structure that exempted the rich from paying taxes. Finally, many progressive elements were eliminated by expulsions and persecutions associated with the Counter Reformation and the Inquisition. Considering further that Spain was deeply involved in Continental struggles, it is no wonder that the economic impact of the colonies was limited. The colonies provided suitably "noble" employment for gentlemen as soldiers and administrators, and a supply of silver (which immediately left Spain to satisfy the pressing claims of bankers from Antwerp to Florence). But there was no enrichment of the Spanish economy, which could not even supply food and manufactured goods to the mines and plantations of America.

This condition not only hurt Spain but also endangered

the very base of Spanish power in the world. Despite very strict laws, Spain had to depend on foreigners to supply such necessities to the colonies and to take away sugar and other products. And here the Dutch, who could outorganize and outtrade anyone and who were not a direct territorial threat, had the inside track. By 1659 they controlled the spice trade and the Brazilian sugar plantations (belonging to Portugal) and were active spoilers in the attempts of the Spaniards (and the British) to keep their colonial trade profitable and monopolized.

The English were, with the French, late entrants in the race, but proved the most successful. At first they were limited to the northern fringes, trying to get some benefit from the frustrating lands of North America, barren of metals and spices and too cold for the growing of sugar cane. As long as the Elizabethan wars lasted, the English could cheer and support the daring privateers who singed the Spanish king's beard, but peace ended the antics of Morgan and Drake. The natural bent of the English was to do as the Dutch did—that is, use their energy as shipbuilders and trading sailors to gain a good share of world commerce—but the Dutch were tough competitors and too much the natural Protestant allies of England to permit a frontal military attack on their trade. Yet in the long run, it was by displacing the Dutch and by acquiring sugar islands in the Caribbean that the English achieved their tremendous mastery of the seas. They combined the commercial skill of the weaker Dutch with the naval power on which Spain had relied, and stood off the intermittent challenge of a French monarchy that was powerful but never fully committed to the sea.

For a long time, the North American colonies were a minor concern in British colonial and commercial policy. They were a refuge for religious dissidents (and insolvent debtors), a convenient source of staples for the sugar plantations, and the scene of modest colonizing ventures. Fish and fur were somewhat profitable, but English interests in these lines were hurt rather than helped by settlement. The sound of the ax was the signal for the trapper to move deeper into the woods, while colonists competed with the English for fish. It is no accident that the North American colonies, particularly the northernmost ones, fitted least well into the colonial system, nor that they broke away near the beginning of the revolutionary economic transformation of Europe.

It is time for us to look at the main currents of international trade around 1700. Two aspects of the complex and rich network deserve special notice. One is the role played by certain ports acting as nodal points for commerce; they imported certain goods for their own hinterland, but also did a large business in reexporting. Thus the prices for many products were determined in London or in Amsterdam, even though the goods were neither produced nor consumed in either place. The other feature is the imbalance between flows to and from given points. The spice and sugar colonies, for example, exported much more (in value terms) than they imported. The difference represented the considerable trading profits reserved to the European traders, the planters' cash balances built up at home, and the costs of carrying and protecting the goods in transit.

The most valuable goods flowing into European ports were, of course, the treasures of the Indies, East and West. From Asia came spices, fine silk and cotton cloth, and the newly fashionable coffee and tea. The Antilles sent sugar, the Carolinas indigo, and Virginia supplied another new fad, tobacco. Europe exported cheap manufactures for the most part: wool cloth, hardware, spirits, weapons, glass. Africa absorbed small amounts of this trade, and in turn supplied gold and ivory for Asia and slaves for the Americas.

The slave trade raised few moral questions in Europe; besides it was very profitable. As we noted in the case of the Roman Empire, slave economies could not normally even maintain their labor supply, whereas the plantations of the New World were growing rapidly. The slavers worked on contract for merchants at home, but it was tempting to crowd in a few additional bodies for the slow journey; and it was always the company's slaves who died, never the captain's.

Other supplies for the plantations came from Europe, luxuries for example, or from New England in the case of barrel staves for molasses and corn meal to feed the hands. The enterprising New Englanders, with their fine timber supplies for building ships, also began to compete with English merchants in the rum and slave trades, but such competition was frowned on by the British government. The northern colonies did export furs and fish, and they were becoming valuable customers for English cloth, tools, weapons, and other amenities of civilized life.

In volume, the largest stream of trade continued to be that between European countries, but it grew less rapidly than the others, and was too varied to allow simple description. The Continental countries often bought their colonial goods through Holland or England, while there was considerable traffic in all directions in raw materials and manufactures: cannon from England and Sweden; fish, grain, and wood from the Baltic; wine from Bordeaux and Cadiz; art goods from France and Italy; wool cloth from England; metals from the German mountains. For we must remember that though transport was still difficult, and governments often uncooperative, techniques of production were primitive. This meant that any one area could produce only a limited range of goods, and people began to look abroad for variety in consumption as their incomes grew.

Governments played a considerable role in the economic life of the mercantile period, both as entrepreneurs and as regulators and controllers of private ventures. In fact, economic activity was scarcely less hampered than under the ubiquitous local regulations and guild restrictions noted in late medieval times. The difference lay mainly in the scale of interference by public power. Increasingly, economic policy was made at the national level. Its ostensible purpose was to encourage and protect national commerce by granting monopoly charters to "companies" and then enforcing these monopolies against foreign and domestic interlopers with all the powers of the state: customs, tax authorities, navy, army, and diplomatic corps. In turn, the companies were supposed to contribute to national prosperity and to the glory of the sovereign. However, it may be helpful to view the last objective as the heart of the matter: instead of considering the mercantilist system as one using the power of the state to encourage trade and economic activity, we can see it as manipulating the economy for the greater power and strength of the crown itself.

A number of puzzling aspects of mercantilist economic policy are much easier to understand with the second approach. Why, for example, was there so much concern with limiting the volume of trade and keeping the profit on each unit very high? After all, this implied making the trade as attractive as possible to outsiders and then working very hard to keep them out. Also, why were policy makers so preoccupied with gold and silver, and so concerned about imports (which required an outflow of metal)? Finally, why the great emphasis on foreign commerce, often to the neglect, or worse, of domestic economic life?

True, the mercantilists had little theoretical knowledge of economic mechanisms, of the *Nature and Causes of the Wealth of Nations,* as Adam Smith called his great book of 1776, but they were not so naive as all that. They realized clearly, for one thing, that no government could prosper simply by milking an economy and doing nothing in return. Even an absolute monarch could not forever squeeze more blood and treasure out of a stagnating country. However, their conception of the appropriate way to encourage the economy was definitely shaped by their concern for the strength and importance of the state.

Now we can see why commerce, especially foreign commerce, was so favored. Since it passed through a few ports it was easy to control. Because foreigners or colonies were involved there was less domestic resistance and a ready excuse for political control, since the safety and honor of the state could be invoked. The protection of trade gave employment to the navy, while sufficiently zealous encouragement of commerce often led to war, so that the army need not stay idle. Finally, the more gold and silver entered the country and remained there, the more was available for the endlessly precarious royal finances.

Admittedly, we are slighting the monetary aspects of economic history somewhat. While money is more than merely a way of keeping track of the quantity of economic activity, it is real goods and services that are the purpose of economic production, and we do not want to lose sight of them. Yet here it is necessary to talk a bit about money and to stress the fallacy behind the mercantilist idea that exports are good and imports bad, that trade is successful when it results in large hoards of precious metals. The reason is not that we want to score debating points against the financiers and ministers of the seventeenth and eighteenth centuries. As I have suggested, their main concern may well have been with the state of the exchequer; and clearly the king could not pay his creditors with lectures on the true causes of his subjects' prosperity. When bills came due or wars had to be financed, gold and silver were needed.

No, the reason for stressing the confusion between real ends and monetary means, of which the mercantilists were often guilty, is that the fallacy has died so hard. It weakened in the nineteenth century, but has revived in the twentieth, buttressed with better arguments than before, and the more dangerous because it contains a real measure of truth.

An inadequate supply of money (and in the days before bank credit money meant specie—gold and silver) could lead to grave difficulties in the economy as well as in the royal finances. Business would stagnate, unemployment increase, and real production suffer. Nor could a country permanently continue to import or spend abroad more than its exports and other sources of specie made it possible to finance. But the basic point of all economic activity, then as now, is to provide a maximum of real goods for consumers and investors. Imports add to the supply and exports detract from it. To forget this, and to place permanent and primary emphasis on precautionary considerations, is to put the cart of means before the horse of purpose.[4]

It was part of the mercantilist system that the colonies were secondary to trade, and in any case intended to serve the mother country. This implied avoiding competition with the home economy in terms of production, an easy matter for the tropical colonies but another thing entirely for Ireland or New England. It also implied that the colonies were expected to pay the costs of "protecting" trade and administering the system. This was politically irksome to the unrepresented Americans, but it was even more galling economically, as they were perfectly aware that they were being "protected" out of a host of profitable trades and manufactures for the greater prosperity of English interests.

The greatest economic sin of mercantilism, however, was its insistence, again in part for fiscal reasons, on limited trade with high profits *for the trader*. As we have emphasized, the limitation of quantity was inseparable from these high profits. Yet it barred the expansion of activity, at both ends of the trade, that was the necessary prelude to sustained economic growth.

Let us consider an example. Suppose, under monopoly, a certain weight of sugar fetched £100 in Barbados and £1000 in Bristol. Now suppose these prices could be changed to £450 and £550, respectively, by opening the trade to competition. The traders might be just as well off despite the greatly reduced margin on each unit, because they would find planters eager to grow, and consumers to buy, much more sugar at the new prices. But the real gainers would be these same planters, whose incomes would rise, and the sweet-toothed English, now able to eat more sugar

---

[4] The problem of raising sufficient revenue for public expenditures was never really solved, but an increasing tax base and recourse to the public at large (rather than just a few financiers) for loans gradually relieved some of the pressure on finance ministers. See Jan Pen, *A Primer on International Trade* (New York: Random House, 1967).

and still have income left over. And there would be additional, indirect beneficiaries, such as the clothiers and farmers of England, who could sell more food and woolen cloth both at home and in the plantations.

In the end, therefore, the markets of Europe and especially North America—troublesome and competitive but large and growing—were the primary factor in helping England achieve the expansion associated with the Industrial Revolution. In comparison, the trade in Eastern luxuries and precious metals was of limited consequence despite its glamor and profits.

By way of conclusion, let us summarize the fortunes of the rival powers in this first great wave of European imperialism. As we have noted, Portugal faded early after having been the leader. She could hang on precariously only to Brazil and Goa. Spain was a much more formidable entry, but her overseas ambitions were incompatible with a stagnant domestic economy. By the seventeenth century, the Spaniards limited their efforts to ensuring the safe arrival in Seville of the two annual treasure convoys from the Americas. The tenuous ties between home and Empire were revealed when the colonies broke away during the Napoleonic Wars. The English, who had already played an increasing part in Latin American trade before independence, consolidated their position afterward. The Monroe Doctrine, though American in expression, was in fact a hands-off warning by Britain to European powers who might challenge that domination.

Holland, relying on organization and efficiency in shipping to compensate for small size, was the least mercantilistic of the powers. For a long time she held a commanding position in trade, but English naval power, together with commercial and industrial growth in Britain, proved too strong in the end. Having been evicted from North America and much of Asia, Holland suffered the final blow from its inclusion in the Napoleonic "Continental System," Napoleon's vain attempt to isolate England from European markets and thus ruin her trade.

Increasingly, the mercantilist rivalry of the eighteenth century became a contest between France and England. France was the larger of the two, and probably the wealthier, but she suffered from serious disadvantages in the maritime and colonial struggle. Colbert's energetic mercantilism, relying heavily on state enterprise as well as control, had not stimulated the private sector to any appreciable extent. In fact, it had probably added to the fiscal pressure that aggravated the sluggishness of the private economy. But this pressure had other causes as well. The social structure, with its relatively sharp division between nobility and bourgeoisie, tended to shield much of the wealth of France both from productive activity and from bearing its share of tax burdens. But the bourgeois themselves seemed more eager to acquire a part of the government's revenues, by purchasing "offices," than to invest in industrial or even commercial enterprises. Social prestige and safety went with royal offices as well as with acquiring land.

Basic to the troubles of France under the *ancien régime* was the parlous state of government finances. This had many causes, including the special privileges of the nobility (and the Church) mentioned above. The lavish court was indeed expensive. But foreign policy probably cost more, and it did not even serve, as the court did, to unify the kingdom by reducing the political role of the nobility. France engaged in ambitious attempts to dominate the Continent, while the maritime and colonial ventures were often too small to be really profitable, but large enough to cost a good deal. In turn, the fiscal difficulties forced the Crown to deal with financiers who made sure of a good personal return on their advances. Finally, the profit opportunities afforded by government finance drew men and capital away from other, more directly productive pursuits, a habit that was to persist in the nineteenth century.

The immediate result of this state of affairs was that

France came out second best in the rivalry with England. A more important consequence, however, was her failure to begin the process of modernization that marked England's economy in the eighteenth century. The French Revolution and the Empire further retarded industrialization, while the return of peace and stability after 1815, strangely enough, had little stimulating effect. But the puzzles of slow French growth will occupy us again in Part II.

There remains England, the most successful nation in the maritime and colonial rivalries of the age. She had many advantages in competing with the other maritime powers, which more than offset the relatively small size (compared to France) and economic backwardness (relative to Holland) of the island nation. As a result of the gradual social transformation of England during the sixteenth and seventeenth centuries, her society became more mobile and her fiscal structure more efficient and just. Most important, perhaps, the English were fully committed to maritime and overseas expansion, and devoted their resources to this end instead of wasting them in costly Continental adventures. The Navy, especially, was carefully developed. So it seems reasonable that England should have prospered under mercantilism, her trade increasing and her political power growing.

Yet the striking difference between England and France in the mercantile age is not relative success *during* the struggle, but what was being prepared in England, namely, the burst of economic transformation and modernization called the Industrial Revolution. And here it seems clear that England's great lead stemmed more from the failures of mercantilism than from its successes, more from the difficulties in implementing restrictive policies than from their results. Let us look for a moment at these difficulties.

Politically, England was much less an absolute monarchy than France, and the control of Parliament over the Crown increased as the seventeenth century and its parade of regimes wore on. Increasingly, legislative power and executive responsibility for administering policy were in the hands of the propertied classes. This was in sharp contrast to the French trend toward a strong central government with a corps of professional civil servants. But while the English propertied classes included the old landed aristocracy, they contained more and more men who were acquiring or consolidating their wealth in all kinds of economic enterprises. Such men might be "improving landlords," merchants, bankers, clothiers, or brewmasters, but they shared a common distaste for the fiscal pressures and economic restrictions characteristic of mercantilist policies. They were as impatient with colonial monopolies and royal regulations as with antiquated guild restrictions; in short they chafed at anything that might interfere with enterprise. To be sure, every monopoly had a monopolist who gained by it, but the general trend was toward lifting the heavy-handed tutelage of the state in economic affairs, particularly at home. Prohibitions and discriminations affecting Ireland or America were more tolerable to Englishmen. In England, where these entrepreneurs had a real say both in making laws and in administering them locally as part-time magistrates and public officers, they tended to abolish restrictions where they could, and largely ignored them in other cases.

The second major problem, as we have seen, was the relative weakness of the tropical colonies as markets for English goods. Yet these plantations were the only ones in which it was possible to sell at monopolistic prices with no fear of competition. For trade and home manufacture to grow, it was necessary for England to exploit the "elasticity" of demand, that is, the opportunity of increasing sales by lowering prices. So, in addition to clamoring for tighter restrictions on competing activity by colonists, the merchants and manufacturers of England agitated to remove irksome restrictions to expansion and technical progress at home. Later, when the American colonies became independent and many of England's important markets were outside her political control, only domestic progress could ensure continued prosperity. But this story belongs in the next part, for it is the essence of England's industrialization.

CHAPTER 7

Achievements
and Limitations
of the Preindustrial
Economy

From the fall of the Roman Empire in the West until somewhere around A.D. 1000, Europe was engaged in the slow process of building a reasonably productive rural economy based on peasant agriculture. Until this process had advanced sufficiently to generate a considerable surplus beyond what was necessary to permit survival, the various manifestations of a surplus, which we call civilization, were limited. They were not absent, to be sure. From the start there were spiritual and temporal powers who lived off the labor of the peasantry, parasites at least in the economic sense. But their wealth was a much more limited part of the total than it had been under the Empire, when ambitious architectural, social, and political structures had been built on a precarious and hard-pressed economic base. The result was that when a more complex economy began to develop again, it was far less fragile and less limited in its effects on people's lives. Most of Europe was in some way affected by the resurgence of commerce and markets, of specialized pro-

duction and urban concentrations. Although the emerging
society was neither just in its political organization nor eq-
uitable in its distribution of income and wealth, there was
not the sharp contrast between slave and freeman, between
city dweller and slave peasant, that had prevailed in antiquity.

We can suggest a parallel between this economic and social progress and the change from the religion of Rome to
that of Christian Europe. Religiously as well as socially,
there was increased concern for the individual, even the
least-favored one, as a full-fledged member of the human
community. Although the medieval serf or industrial
worker might be exploited and tyrannized, he was never
considered merely an instrument for the private use of a
king or a church, or even of his lord. The great monuments
of Europe were not tombs for dead Pharoahs, not temples
for gods and their priests, but churches in which the people
worshiped. This current of individualism was to grow after
the Middle Ages, marked by great intellectual movements
such as the Reformation and the Enlightenment, and by
increasing freedom and diversity in economic institutions
and enterprises. Even when societies became highly interdependent and their economic problems too large to dispense
with collective action, the primacy of the individual and the
community over the leadership would be maintained, often
in practice and nearly always in professions of legitimacy.

The rural economy of Europe slowly organized to make
use of its growing surpluses. We have seen how improved
techniques and greater stability permitted the rise of a
panoply of new economic forms: fairs and towns, banks
and workshops, guilds and companies. Production and consumption were more and more separated, though not completely in comparison to what was to come. It was an un-
even process, but it could not be reversed except temporarily
and locally. Perhaps its very slowness made it more powerful.
Compared with antiquity, and also with much of the more
recent economic development in non-European countries, it
appears that Europe expanded its economic production rela-

tively strongly before committing itself to a very complex and interdependent exchange economy.[5]

A part of the reason for this pattern lay in the role of forces that retarded for a time the growth of trade in Europe but then finally favored it. We have mentioned the invaders of the early Middle Ages, the enterprising but aggressive Saracens and Vikings, who accentuated Europe's isolation before they contributed to breaking it. There remains the role of the Church, which was also curiously ambiguous.

We saw earlier how the Church had preserved some of the towns from total disappearance and had acted as the guardian of technical knowledge in turbulent and unlettered times. Through the Peace of God and through the highly organized and stable monasteries, powerful stimuli were provided to production and commerce. Yet the Church never wearied of pointing out the spiritual dangers of economic activity, especially that which was successful enough to banish direct and literal concern with "daily bread."

There were three basic ethical problems raised by economic activity involving large enterprises or concentrated wealth, and they preoccupied the Church and its reformers, as well as the faithful, at least until the eighteenth century.

One important moral question was the propriety of becoming too involved in the things of this world to the detriment of concern with the next. So long as man worked from sunup to sundown to keep alive, there was little the Church could do, but what of the merchant who pondered ways of adding one more stack of gold coins to those he was in the process of counting? A second difficulty lay in the contradiction between the asceticism and discipline central to Christian virtue and the possibilities for enjoyment opened up by wealth. Could they be reconciled, or perhaps separated, so that economic success would not lead to moral degradation through self-indulgence? Finally, there was the contradiction between the selfishness inherent in acquiring exclusive

[5] The income per inhabitant of Western European countries at the end of the preindustrial period was much higher—perhaps by a factor of two—than today's level in many nations, such as Pakistan or Algeria, attempting modern economic development.

right to economic goods and the obligations of Christian charity. It seemed clear that I could get more only by leaving less for you, my brother.

In the Middle Ages, the Church proposed a consistent answer to these problems for its own communities and a much less coherent one for the faithful. In the monastery, discipline, collective life, and total commitment to spiritual concerns eliminated the problems. The monks could work hard and effectively, and the monastery could be a model of economic efficiency, with no necessity for religious duties to be slighted or vows of poverty to be broken. The surplus could further the work of the Church elsewhere, could be expended in glorifying God through Art, or could be distributed to the poor. Laymen, subject to less rigorous and continuous religious direction, faced greater conflicts. They were exhorted to limit their concern for accumulation and consumption, to remember the Lord in their dealings either with His Church or with His children, and especially were enjoined from charging more than the "just price" or lending money at interest. Yet there were fundamental contradictions in all this. The urge to accomplish could not simply be proclaimed a satanic force, nor the thrifty and skillful workman less virtuous than his shiftless neighbor. More important, as economic life became more complex and people's activities more interdependent, it became increasingly difficult to live according to the simple "family" model of the economy envisaged by the Church rules.

When a man grew grain, and fed his workmen, it was easy to determine a "fair" wage—for instance, by sharing the crop in some reasonable way. And if a laborer was ill, he must be advanced enough to tide him over, without asking him to pay back more than he had received. But what was the just price for grain sold in a far-off market? Why prohibit interest on money advanced to a rich merchant to finance another profitable voyage? Most important of all, perhaps, the basic assumption that economic success was at the *expense* of one's brethren became more and more dubious. Great merchants made for prosperous towns, efficient clothiers provided more employment than unenterprising ones, and rich financiers could advance funds in time of famine or promote large and useful ventures for the common good. Something like the modern theory of markets, in which prices act as signals and promote mutually beneficial exchanges so long as they are not too badly rigged, was being worked out, though obscurely. Finally, the doctrine was being ignored in practice, by private men as well as by princes, not least those of the Church itself.

The men who tried to reform the Catholic Church and eventually founded separate sects were more concerned with the obvious discrepancies between practice and doctrine within the Church than they were with the inherent contradictions in that doctrine. They were not interested in providing an ethic for an affluent society, or one in which great enterprises would make possible, and perhaps necessary, great concentrations of economic power and wealth. Yet their disciples often turned out to be men who were especially active in the new ways. They evolved what has come to be known as the Protestant Ethic, another set of answers to the problems inherent in trying to reconcile God and Mammon.

It is important to note that the new ethic did not deny, especially at first, the spiritual hazards of pursuing and holding wealth. Even in the eighteenth century, John Wesley despaired of effecting any permanent moral reform among the poor, because he saw that virtue would make them industrious, industry make them prosperous, and prosperity lead again to vice. But the Protestants did evolve a way out, which we can try to sketch, with the warning that this is one of the great debates in the history of ideas, and that it admits of no simple summary acceptable to everyone.

In brief, man was seen as having to fight the good fight *in* an evil world, rather than by renouncing it. Moreover, he must do it largely by himself, with the help of God's grace, and must not therefore be much influenced by the standards of others. Being dependent on himself, he had to have a function in the world, something that permitted him to

hold his own. This was his *calling*. The man touched by
divine grace was especially favored in having a strong calling, and it was his duty to cultivate his gifts and, therefore,
to be successful.

In this way, economic activity acquired an ethical justification and motivation of its own, over and above the acqui-
sition of worldly goods. A man could logically pursue success and at the same time avoid luxury or ostentation in
consumption, and, in particular, return his profits to the
business, whether farm or manufacture. It was also logical
for him to accept only rules of behavior that fitted in with
the necessities of his economic calling, and to reject any interference with it on the part of church or government. In
the end, the only way of reconciling individual responsibility and initiative with the interdependence of complex economic activity was through free markets. Remove all ethical
and personal connotations from buying and selling, from
pricing and production. Friendship, duty, charity, patriotism, piety, all these have nothing to do with economic activity, and any interference in their name will lead only to
distortions, thus making everyone worse off. Convenience
demands some standards of behavior, a code of commercial
morality, but the main rule is self-interest: *caveat emptor*.

The short step to complete absence of any moral control
over economic activity was taken in the nineteenth century
by many businessmen. Of course, these men often had high
moral standards in their private lives, but in their profession they were bound only by the duty to be successful and
by the accepted code of the trade. Since markets supposedly
worked for everyone's benefit, any interference with their
free play was considered reprehensible. Further, society had
no right to criticize or control conditions of work, income
distribution, or business cycles. Finally, in the twentieth
century we have gone a step farther. Virtue and faith are
often viewed as valuable primarily because they promote
success in economic life.

After this long parenthesis on religion in economic life, we return to our summary. The commercial development of the Middle Ages had been accompanied by further technical progress in agriculture and industry, and had made this progress possible by enlarging markets. Yet in the centuries after 1500, commercial expansion continued with relatively minor changes in the productive capacity of the European economies. Because of overseas expansion and of the new markets and resources it made available, capacity limitations did not become serious for a long time.

Yet in comparing Europe in 1750 with the same area today, one is struck by how much greater recent economic change has been in some areas than in others. Whereas by 1750 markets and specialization were already highly developed, industry was primitive and agriculture shackled by the problem of soil fertility. Sea transport was so far ahead of land carriage that New York and London had easier contact than Paris and Basle. There was a striking (to us) contrast between the commercial importance and sophistication of the English cloth trade, say, and the tiny cottages in which each step of production was so laboriously carried out, by hand, on a small quantity of wool.

Before beginning our account of the Industrial Revolution and of the larger subject of economic development, we should recognize that bottlenecks did restrict greater productivity in eighteenth-century Europe. Some were physical, all somehow involving the inability of man to multiply his strength sufficiently. Wood was scarce for fuel, and inadequate for building more ambitious tools. The soil, as we have seen, balked at feeding ever-increasing numbers. Transport was hindered by the lack of strength to lay down good roads cheaply, by the energy required to pull heavy loads, and by the primitive vehicles available. Yet many of the problems were man-made too. Society was, as we have seen, not primarily organized for economic activity, particularly not that which required great mobility or vast concentrations of resources.

In the next century and a half, social institutions and

techniques would change together, giving rise to a system that seemed as coherent in the later nineteenth century as the manorial system may have appeared a millennium before. Only now the rhythm of contradictions and stresses was much more rapid, so that the system of industrial capitalism was already being challenged and changed, while it was still very young and comparatively undeveloped. In Europe especially, it was a close race between an apocalyptic confrontation of opposing forces and the very beginning of the industrialization process in regions and countries left out of the earlier push.

We must, however, again simplify, and consider the growth process first in the abstract and then in various countries. In Chapters 15 and 16 we shall turn to the contradictions that rent industrial Europe, especially from 1900 onward, and then look at the remarkable phoenix emerging from the ashes of World War II.

PART II 〜〜〜〜〜

ECONOMIC
DEVELOPMENT
IN EUROPE

CHAPTER 8 〰〰〰

The Concept of
Economic Development

The emphasis of this book is on economic growth, that is, the increase over time of the quantity of goods and services available to the members of a society. It is a doubly appropriate theme in a book devoted to the economic history of Europe and written in the 1960s. For the increase in material wealth is not only the most striking characteristic of Western societies in the last two centuries, but also today's chief political problem and the goal of national communities everywhere. And the cradle of economic growth, the region in which men were able for the first time to break through the barriers that seemed to limit their productive capacity to a level perilously close to the line between survival and extinction, was Europe, Western Europe in particular.

As we have seen, preindustrial Europe was capable of economic progress, but such progress was neither rapid nor sustained. The two limitations were linked, the key variable being population growth. As Malthus pointed out, improvements in the standard of living of the population as a whole had more drastic repercussions on the number of people than on the possibilities for further increases in output. The major change that later took place in Europe was a reversal of the relative magnitudes of these effects. So we can define an economy capable of *modern* economic growth as one in which improvements in productivity increase the capacity of the economy to produce by more than they increase the number of people who lay claim to the output.

We should note several things about this definition. First, it assumes that the major force making for economic growth is, in fact, economic growth; in other words, that the process is essentially a self-reinforcing one. Second, it forces us to look at an economy in a complex way, focusing on the relationship between trends over time rather than simply measuring incomes or capital stock or attaching labels to institutional systems. Finally, it leads us inevitably to focus on a transition, on the period in which the economy reverses the relative force of trends in output and claimants. This transition, with its preparation and consolidation, we call *economic development*. We shall look briefly at the basic process of economic growth and then at the characteristic differences between the progressive economy and the backward or premodern one, and finally try to gain some insight into the mysterious transition, the development process itself.

At this point it should hardly be necessary to warn the reader that we are dealing with a controversial subject. The enormous difficulties of non-Western nations in trying to transform their economies in our time bear ample witness to our lack of full answers. Indeed, the trouble starts even before we say anything at all about the requirements for development. It begins when we define the process itself. We are implicitly assuming that the two kinds of economies, developed and undeveloped, are homogeneous enough categories to be worth distinguishing, and that passing from one to the other is a one-time process with substantially uniform properties. Yet the economies involved are very different

—are we talking about 1800 or 1950? We cannot entirely avoid these strong assumptions, but we will hedge. In particular, we shall try to point out variations on the general theme arising from the particular characteristics of individual economies, and we shall also make room for incomplete transformations and for cases requiring more than one transition to keep economic growth going or to restart it.

One essential of the growth process is *investment,* that is, withholding a substantial part of present economic surplus to increase the future output of the economy. Investment is basically a simple process, if only one takes the trouble to focus on essentials and avoids the distraction of various institutional instruments and symbols, such as money, stocks, and so forth.

Goods can serve two purposes: satisfying immediate wants or ensuring more production later. The alternative uses of a potato for seed or food provide a simple example, but we can also think of the alternative uses of a man's labor to make a shirt to wear or a sail for his fishing boat. The capacity to produce tomorrow depends on the amount of output we hold back today. Thus, investment involves abstention and waiting: some of today's real goods are not consumed, and the counterpart (in terms of more goods) becomes available later (the amount of the counterpart being dependent on the length of the wait).

Very closely tied to investment is *knowledge,* the other major factor in growth. Though there is no apparent reason why an economy should be unable to keep plowing back enough of its output to stay permanently ahead of population growth with unchanged techniques of production, this approach turns out in fact to be a hopeless one. It is also necessary to get more output out of each unit of resources that contributes to the output, whether human labor, the riches of earth and sea, or the output held back in past times, which we call capital.

Economically significant knowledge takes several forms. One is better techniques, embodied particularly in new equipment. Another is information about opportunities, related to the joining and enlarging of markets. Last, and certainly not least, is the quality of labor, the training and skills vested in people. This ranges from literacy and practice in doing a simple job to the most complex professional or technical qualifications.

Investment (or capital formation) and increased knowledge are very closely related, since each advance in knowledge implies more investment. It takes real resources to develop new methods and to inform people of their existence, while the new techniques are of no use until we build equipment that embodies them. Finally, training and education require teachers and facilities, not to mention the output lost because people are learning to be more productive later instead of producing as best they can right now. We shall find in developing and developed countries not only more investment, but also a greater share of that investment going to the production of knowledge. This last fact, especially, explains why growth has not tended to slow down, as pessimists often feared it would.

Comparing the progressive, or growing, economy with the undeveloped one is like looking at two photographs marked "before" and "after." The comparison is instructive, but does not, by itself, tell us much about how to get from one to the other. The reason is that development is a process, not a series of changes that can take place independently of one another and in any order. To use a cooking analogy, the difference is that between a recipe on the one hand and a list of ingredients plus a photograph of the result on the other. I stress this because the fallacy often has serious practical consequences, particularly today when development is an urgent goal of public policy. Too many people fasten on some property of developed economies and want to graft this feature onto an undeveloped one without further ado. Examples of such fallacious reasoning are numerous. A developed country usually employs few people in agriculture, so that sector is neglected in favor of industry, the mark of the progressive economy. Or, it is suggested, advanced countries use highly automatic machines and produce a very wide variety of goods, so why should the country trying to develop have to specialize and make do with simpler equipment? Perhaps it should not, but you cannot tell simply by comparing the two economies.

With this warning, how does development change an economy? One major difference, obviously, is that the developed economy has a greater accumulation of capital. This means more machinery, bigger and sturdier buildings, trained labor, more use of energy for economic tasks, all the well-known marks of an industrial society. But agriculture is not neglected, since it is smaller only in comparison with the other sectors of the economy and much larger, usually, in the absolute amount of output per inhabitant.

Yet we want to focus on two less graphic and more abstract changes. One is the increased reliance on markets, with its concomitants of specialization, interdependence, and large-scale production. This helps, not only because large-scale production is efficient, but also because producing for a large market increases the likelihood of competitors, who are as vital to improved efficiency as the technical requisites of scale and investment. The second property characteristic of a developed economy is *mobility*. This has many dimensions, social as well as material. Obviously, goods and people must move more quickly and more cheaply, but information, ideas, and patterns of behavior also have to be more mobile. For change is not only frequent in a developed economy—*it is the necessary condition for continued progress.*

Mobility provides us with a clue to the real drama of development, the "scandal," as one writer put it. The progressive economy makes mobility relatively painless for individuals and social groups. They are used to it, and the material costs and uncertainties can more easily be borne or protected against. But when the development process begins, it imposes a degree of mobility that strikes the more rigid pre-modern society as an upheaval. The need to change, like the need to invest, is now; the rewards of change, like the greater productivity made possible by more capital, lie in an inherently uncertain future. So we shall be particularly concerned, in reviewing the various countries and their development, with the problem of mobility. How rigid was the society before development? How much upheaval did the particular historical circumstances impose? How strong was the resistance to change?

In the transition itself, we shall focus on one central dilemma evolving from the need, but also from the impossibility, of doing everything at once. As we have seen, development is a process, and all parts of the economy interact. But the progressive forces, the specialists and the capital, are all painfully scarce at first. Should they be thinly spread, at the risk of being overcome by the resistance to change, or should they be concentrated at a few points, hoping somehow that the rest of the society and the economy will follow or be dragged along? This will be our other major concern in studying the various countries. How concentrated was the initial push? How difficult was it to extend development from its initial centers to the bulk of economic life? Did the consolidation prove as difficult, or perhaps more so, than the initial transformation?

Thus we are left with a compromise between the social scientist's desire to present a unified picture and the historian's obligation to note and preserve the variety of experience. Economic development is a process, but it has no single rigid rule for success. Initial conditions, environment, national character perhaps, historical accident too, all these modify and condition what occurs. But certain things must occur, in one way or another and to a greater or lesser extent, and the particular features of early stages affect the later ones.

Now let us leave abstract generalization and return to Europe in the eighteenth century—in this case, England. We shall consider the conditions for development and the changes that took place during the great transformation, both in and out of industry. England will prove a special case, because its development was patterned on no other, but we shall see that history knows only special cases.

CHAPTER 9

Economic Development
in England:
The Elements

In the early 1760s, England emerged from a period of war abroad and agricultural depression at home into a time of economic prosperity. There had been many such "booms" in English history, and this one portended nothing exceptional, the more so as the economy had not been all that sharply depressed. Yet this upswing, it would turn out, was unlike any of its predecessors. Although there would again be depressions and hard times, the basic rhythm of economic growth had undergone a profound change. Increases of 1 percent or more a year in the total volume of goods and services (what men did not yet call gross national product) were nothing new. What was new was that this growth became a trend rather than a temporary spurt, a trend pressing on for decades, indeed for two centuries, with no signs of permanent slowing down.

One percent a year, even 2, seems a modest kind of revolution. But this neglects the cumulative effects of change at a constant rate, that is, where the absolute amount of increase itself goes up over time. Thus, if the per capita income of England was £60 ($144) a year in 1760 (in today's prices that is a fair guess), and the rate of growth of that income a modest 1 percent a year, each Englishman would have £120 to spend in 1830 and £240 in 1900. By this time his income would be increasing by $6 every year instead of the less than $2 increase he would have received in 1760. Moreover, the effects of increased income on the standard of living are more impressive than the figures would suggest, since many basic needs, such as the need for food in particular, increase slowly in relation to income.

Nevertheless, while there were real effects for most people's material lives and considerable changes for many who profited especially, it was the rhythm of economic and social life that was most drastically changed by the Industrial Revolution. Instead of a precarious stability, there was now dangerous but promising change. It affected consumption, occupations, location, the countryside people looked at, and the social forces shaping their lives. Perhaps most important in the long run was the expectation of future progress and ceaseless change now built into a system that penalized those who attached overwhelming importance to hanging on while it favored the more adaptable.

It is convenient to see the great change beginning around 1760 as the result of a number of distinct, although not independent, evolutions in various sectors of the economy. In this chapter we shall examine the changes that combined to produce a mutation. Although it has been called the Industrial Revolution, a term that we would be pedantic and pretentious to discard, the transformation of Britain depended on many elements besides new techniques and organizational forms in the manufacturing sector. Moreover, just as the word "industrial" neglects much of what happened, so too the term "revolution" can give a misleading impression. As we shall see, the modernization of Britain depended on factors maturing for more than two hundred years, while on the other hand at least a century passed after 1760 before the premodern elements in the English economy were relegated to a clearly subordinate role.

In order to understand the complex changes in English agriculture that came to a head during this stage of development and that are closely related to the opening up of England's social structure, we must go back to the fifteenth century. England, like the rest of Europe, was then recovering from the depopulation wrought by famine, war, and plague in the previous period. Men were scarce and land correspondingly abundant. Landlords seeking tenants to work their fields were forced to give long leases and to content themselves with modest rents. The prosperity of the sixteenth century, accompanied by a fall in the value of money (i.e., a rise in prices), made the rents even lower in terms of real goods or man-years of labor. In addition, the boom enriched many merchants. The result was a great loosening of the market for land. Many people were able for the first time to buy land, so that a new class of proprietors, small squires or townspeople, joined the traditional classes of nobles and peasants.

This new class of proprietors did not merely buy land, however. They *invested* in land, and the investment was profitable only if the land could be made to yield a sizable surplus over the cost of working. Nor were the traditional landholders left out of the heightened concern for production and profit, since the fall in rents endangered their economic status. As a result, there was a strong push to do away with the antiquated institutions and methods of traditional agriculture that hindered innovation as well as adaptation to the changing requirements and opportunities offered by growing markets. The most notable mark of rationality and change was the enclosure movement.

To enclose land meant to turn the fact of individual property into a physical and economic reality. As we have seen in our discussions of the medieval manor, the early agricultural holdings were divided, in terms of legal rights, among a number of people, but the whole estate was a unit from the point of view of running it as a farm, with its three open fields, its woods and commons, and its various buildings. When an estate was enclosed a fresh start was made. Every "owner," including those who had tenure rights as landholding serfs, was allowed to claim his share of the estate, but he was given one piece of land rather than various rights to several parts. The result was to transform the estate into a number of compact farms, and usually the owners delimited their new holding with a fence or hedgerow, or other "enclosure."

What were the consequences of this reapportionment? First, a number of marginal people, who had eked out a living from their cottage, their garden, and the few animals they were allowed to let run on common land, but who had no formal rights to any plowed land, were completely eliminated as landholders. Unless they could find work as servants or wage laborers, they were forced to leave. The second, and more purely economic, consequence was to free landowners from any restrictions on farming practice. They could now use their land or sell out, try new methods or stick to the old. In particular, the economic forces of division of labor and of markets now had a much more direct influence.

From the social point of view, much has been written about enclosure, often by people who considered it as a measure of expropriation of the peasantry by the gentry or as a way of providing cheap labor for industry. As we shall see, the effects on agricultural population came more from the particular economic changes made possible by enclosure than from the change in agrarian patterns directly. For the fact is that enclosure was, by and large, carried out with great fairness. To be sure, it worked to the advantage of large landowners, or at least substantial "yeomen," but this was a result of the familiar law of production that efficiency requires scale. Moreover, many peasants who could not claim enough land to put together a viable farm found they could work sufficiently large holdings as tenants, while others found employment for wages, either in agriculture or elsewhere.

Change is hard, and for the poor—lacking any savings to tide them over and without the knowledge and skills to seek and hold alternative jobs—it can be catastrophic. Moreover, the enclosure procedure observed formal rights more effectively than customary ones, while the powerful position of the squire could often impose the decision to enclose even if he did not affect the actual division of land. But enclosure helped many smaller men in addition to the dominant descendant of the manorial lord, and the work was done impartially and carefully under Parliamentary supervision. Finally, the process was drawn out over centuries. It began strongly in the fifteenth and sixteenth centuries, continued at a reduced pace through the seventeenth and early eighteenth centuries (there was considerable official as well as private opposition to the practice), and reached a climax, during the spurt of development itself, from 1795 to 1815.

Agriculture in enclosed areas could be, as we have said, more responsive to market conditions. In the sixteenth century, for example, the prosperity of the wool trade made sheep grazing profitable, while the shortage of manpower tended to discourage the growing of crops. The result was that enclosed lands tended to be converted from arable to pasture, with a corresponding decrease in employment. Hence the fear of rural depopulation. Around 1800, on the contrary, the rise in the price of grain, due to war and the effects of industrialization, caused a sharp increase in the area devoted to crops, and brought a lively demand for labor. At that time, enclosure was pushed as a means of freeing former wasteland and commons from the grazing rights of the community so that they could be plowed up.

In between, a more complex and drawn-out change had slowly been spreading through English agriculture, tending to break the vicious circle of preindustrial agriculture of which we have spoken earlier. Agricultural productivity had previously been limited by inadequate fertilization of the soil, preventing the growing of sufficient fodder for the animals who provided the necessary fertilizing elements. The new method consisted of integrating animal husbandry with the growing of vegetable crops, using a rotation in which fodder crops, such as legumes, clover, and turnips, replaced fallow, that is, periods of idleness for the soil. The new agriculture was especially suited to light, chalky, upland soils, formerly considered inferior. The result was that wastelands, once they were enclosed, provided some of the most productive farming areas. The clay soils on which most of England's crops had been grown were enclosed less rapidly, and slowly shifted over to mixed dairy and crop farming, often in smallish holdings with less than the latest technology.

Here we find a pattern, characteristic of the development process in England, which we shall encounter again in the textile industry. Instead of achieving a major change in existing practice, it proved much easier to by-pass the strongholds of the old and to establish almost a new agriculture on other soils, particularly in the eastern part of England. The more traditional farmers of the West and North often obtained employment in the industries that happened to find congenial locations primarily in those regions; or they slowly lost ground in the competitive struggle, finally sinking, after about 1875, into a depression from which there was to be no relief except migration to the town (or government subsidies in the twentieth century for the remaining few).

Thus, the close connection between land tenure and social structure was loosened, if not immediately broken. Land became an asset among others, an investment competing with commercial or industrial ventures, to be acquired or sold as seemed economically appropriate. Similarly, agriculture became more nearly an occupation like others, rather than a way of life to be pursued irrespective of its economic desirability. To be sure, the changes were less than abrupt. Landownership still brought important social and political advantages, but these advantages no longer relieved men of the concern for getting the best possible economic return from their property. This concern had important consequences for the economic development of England. Very often, the largest and most aristocratic proprietors took the lead in introducing new methods, while the considerable profits they derived from well-managed lands enabled them to finance costly investments in canals, roads, mines, and other enterprises. Similarly, merchants could transfer the profits from their commerce to the land, and contribute to agricultural improvement while covering up the somewhat crass origins of their fortune with a patina of landed gentility.

The agrarian transformation of England had as profound an impact on the poor as it did on the rich, particularly as it affected their numbers. As we have mentioned, in preindustrial times the size of the population was limited by the availability of land. In part, the dismal mechanism of insufficient food with its grim consequences of famine and disease choked off sustained increases in the number of people. However, the birth rate was affected as strongly as the death rate. At a time when men died young and when infant mortality tended to be greater than the rate of surviving births, early marriage was necessary for a growing population. The age of marriage in turn depended on the availability of land holdings.

In the course of the eighteenth century the picture changed. A man no longer needed to inherit a small farm in order to marry, and indeed small independent farms were diminishing in importance. On the other hand, increasing opportunities for renting land appeared, especially for a young man willing to apply the new methods being pushed by progressive landlords. For others, many more jobs for wages became available, either in agriculture, in towns, or in domestic industry. The last was especially important, for it enabled a man to derive real benefit from his family. Cottage industry was really a tiny private enterprise employing the whole family, even if the merchant commanded its activity as rigorously as any boss.

The result of agricultural progress and increased industrial activity was that a temporary burst of population increase, the normal reaction to a presumed fall in the early eighteenth century, was transformed into a long-term gap between rates of birth and death. Like the growth of production, the gap was modest in terms of annual increments —little more than 1 percent—but its cumulative effects were considerable. Britain's population grew from some 7½ million in 1751 to 16½ million in 1831 and 21 million in 1851, partly due to Irish immigration.

At first, it seems, the gap was due more to sustained high births and the disappearance of sharp peaks in mortality than to any great decline in the normal death rate. Improvements in diet, sanitation, medical care, and housing, which the Industrial Revolution would in time bring within the reach of most people, were still largely promises. Nevertheless, the picture we have formed of terrible hardships in the early days of industrialization and agricultural upheaval is not borne out by the demographic statistics. It is not so much that the early factories and industrial towns were less ghastly than we imagine. Rather, we have tended to picture preindustrial England as far more pleasant than it was. Towns were firetraps, with open sewers and no semblance of a clean water supply or adequate food preservation. Country cottages were cold, damp, often windowless hovels, and the diet of the rural poor was even less regular and balanced than in towns. Finally, an element of mystery persists in the story of European population in the eighteenth century. After centuries of recurrent epidemics, of which the Black Plague in the mid-fourteenth century was only one episode, these terrible illnesses vanished for all practical purposes. Why, we do not know, except that neither the beginnings of modern medical science nor the slow increases in the standard of living are plausibly adequate explanations.

People represent both mouths to feed and arms to work.

The Industrial Revolution in England was favored by brisk growth of demand for the increasing output of farms and workshops. A rising population contributed to this situation, as did the fast-growing overseas markets whose development we have traced in Chapter 8. Yet demand depends not only on the number of people, but also on their tastes and incomes, and on the way production is adapted to them. England proved to have a combination conducive to sustained effective demand. Despite the existence of rich and poor, and even perhaps a growing disparity between them, wealth and income were evenly distributed compared to the structure of other countries, while the average income seems even in 1750 to have been higher in England than in Continental countries. The result was brisk demand for the kind of ordinary everyday goods the British seemed to be good at making, articles that were cheap and practical even if the French sneered at their commonness or lack of beauty. These prosaic cottons, potteries, pans, buckles, and needles, because they could be made in large numbers with primitive machines, set into motion a great cumulative process of investment, production, efficiency, and profit (leading to more investment), which then carried the economy to its industrial and commercial predominance.

What of the manpower, the labor force needed in the first factories, the fields, and the shops? How can we reconcile the vast "reserve army" of men supposedly driven from the fields by enclosure with the pitiful sight of small children toiling in the mills? As we have seen, the late eighteenth century in fact found agriculture clamoring for "hands," while recurrent wars further stretched the supply of able-bodied men. There were other reasons, however, why women and children were employed, particularly in the textile industries. One relates to our previous point about the real nature of the Industrial Revolution in England. We tend to see it as largely concerned with the cotton industry, whereas many other activities, together several times as large as the cotton industry ever became, grew and clamored for male labor. In addition to agriculture, there was heavy industry, mining and metallurgy in particular, and also the huge effort entailed in construction: houses, roads, canals, factory buildings, docks.

But it is a point that mill owners often preferred women and children. They were paid less, for a start, and were often better suited for jobs requiring nimble fingers rather than strong backs. In addition, they seem to have proved more amenable to the new pattern of work imposed by the factory system. It is hard for us to realize just how alien the regular, machine-regulated and whistle-timed factory discipline was to men who had grown up in the fields or in a cottage-workshop. There, although the hours worked per year might be just as long, the scheduling was much less rigid. When the harvest had to be brought in or when the merchant had supplied wool, every daylight hour was used for days at a time. But when a job was done, there would be a three-day rest, with two more to recover from the "rest." Furthermore, a man liked to impose a human rhythm on work, whereas the machine would not stop, slow down, or even speed up to get the job done.

In addition to labor, economic activity requires capital. We have asserted that investment is the heart of the growth process. Yet we shall say little about capital in English economic development. Of course there was investment, though here again most of it took place in agriculture and transport, and only slowly were really great sums required for industry. How is it that capital seems to have been such a secondary problem? How could industry develop with no great new institutions for channeling the savings of the economy into the new activities?

There are several answers, but whether they overexplain the problem or fail to eliminate our ignorance, it is hard to say. Somehow, the capital was there. The great landowners and merchants had a large share in financing some of the biggest enterprises, especially the canals and docks that united the English market and joined it to the world. Then there were a host of smaller men—squires, merchants, or professional men, who could be talked into putting up a few hundred or thousand pounds for a venture. For expansion and innovation were in the air, while the early industrial enterprises were modest. The machines seem unimpressive to us and were cheap by the standards of their day. Later on, capital came mainly from within the business, profits prudently reinvested by the owner, who was far more interested in the success of the business than in buying luxuries he had no leisure to enjoy. His sons and grandsons, born to prosperity and affluence, would not always put the interests of the business first.

Labor, capital, and raw materials provided the ingredients for industrial production, but there was also an essential human element, the entrepreneur.[1] It was the entrepreneur's job to organize all these factors, to assume the risk of committing resources in the hope of selling goods at a profit later, and to manage the business through teething troubles, depressions, and the many problems posed by changing conditions. Though seldom an inventor himself, the entrepreneur had to innovate, that is, apply and adapt the inventions of others and work out new solutions to new problems.

Clearly, the rewards were great enough, in eighteenth- and nineteenth-century England, to call forth a great many such men. It is surprisingly difficult to say much about their origins. Few if any came from the extremes of the social scale, but they were a varied lot in every social and economic dimension. Artisans, merchants, farmers, professionals, all were represented in the class of manufacturers who would play such a great part in Victorian England. The very diversity of their origins testifies to the considerable openness of English society.

Although the entrepreneurs were faced with a host of new

[1] Whereas Marx emphasized the role of capital accumulation and markets, Joseph Schumpeter explicitly made the entrepreneur the hero of the economic development story.

problems in setting up factory industry based on mechanization, large scale, and untried techniques, they were helped by well-established traditions. Commerce and markets were almost second nature to the English. Moreover, the middle classes, more numerous than elsewhere, enjoyed greater social status than on the Continent. A major reason for this was the inheritance system, based on primogeniture—the undivided right of the eldest son to his father's property. Not only did this prevent agricultural land from being cut up in each generation, as was done, for instance, in France, but it provided a constant downward stream of new recruits for the middle class, men who were gentlemen by birth and education, but who could not rely on inherited wealth or position. Many, it is true, went into the liberal professions, into the services, or into politics and letters. But there was little stigma attached to "trade," that is, to the pursuit of wealth in industry or commerce. Finally, England had known industry before the eighteenth century. It had been modest in its methods and size compared with what was coming, but the problem of adaptation was far less acute than it is in a truly agrarian society trying to shift suddenly to an industrial pattern.

The Industrial Revolution is synonymous with new manufacturing techniques, even though we have seen that the story has many other aspects. It has been traditional to see England's development as largely due to a spate of inventions, particularly in cotton, iron, and the use of steam. Clearly these were necessary, for expansion with the traditional tools and sources of energy would soon have become impossible. Cottage industry, dependent on human strength, was inherently inefficient, since the only way of expanding was to hire more cottagers, each equipped with the same loom, grinding wheel, or wool combs. But the greatest bottleneck seems to have been energy, as evidenced by a growing crisis in the supply of wood. The wood short-

age became a national emergency when the navy clamored
for more ships, but wood had so many roles in the preindustrial economy that its scarcity affected every sector.

We shall consider first the ways in which wood was displaced as a fuel and a construction material, then the transport revolution, and finally the cotton industry, where the
other advances found their first great use.

The English had long known the use of coal. As wood
became scarce, more and more industries turned to the black
substance, as did householders for cooking and heating. The
biggest users were in the process industries: brewers, bakers,
glassmakers, potters, dyers. There were, however, two major
limitations. Coal, like wood, could provide only heat but no
mechanical energy, and it seemed impossible to use it as a
fuel in the smelting of iron. The first problem was solved
through the development of the steam engine; the second
yielded to the long efforts of iron men unaided by scientific
knowledge of the chemical processes involved in ferrous
metallurgy.

Steam engines, or fire pumps as they were first called, were
in use half a century before James Watt was even born. The
early ones were crude devices, mainly used for pumping
water from mines. The vacuum formed by steam cooling in
a closed space provided the pumping force. These engines
were inefficient, mainly because the cylinder had to be
heated and cooled at every stroke, but this presented few
problems in mines, where fuel was there for the taking.
Watt's great contribution was to provide a separate chamber
for condensing the steam, thereby conserving most of the
heat and economizing greatly on the use of fuel. In addition, he and Boulton, who first manufactured the Watt engines, made many technical improvements to increase their
usefulness.

It is good to pause and stress the importance of such improvements, for they often make the difference between an
ingenious idea for a science museum and an economically
significant device or process. The steam engine, for example,
though we think of it as belonging to the first industrial age,

has continued to be improved ever since the 1780s, when Watt and Boulton sold their first models. Economic progress did not come from *the* steam engine, important as the invention was. It was greatly assisted by thousands of steam engines, of all sizes and types, which could vastly increase the power available to all sorts of enterprises, from textile mills to railroad engines. This helps us understand why countries have remained so different in their economic development. Inventions travel easily. What is harder to import is the capacity to perfect, produce, diffuse, and then use new techniques in the quantity and variety needed for the manifold tasks and conditions of a specific economy.

The steam engine could have been neither built nor used to any extent without great increases in the supply of iron. Until the eighteenth century, iron of reasonable purity could be produced only with the use of charcoal, partly because coal contained too many impurities and partly because the use of coal required smelting temperatures higher than were obtainable. The use of coke, that is, coal freed of foreign matter by controlled burning, dates back to the early years of the century, although the new method spread slowly. The difficulty was that certain procedures and qualities of raw materials were necessary to make it work, and there was no way of specifying these quantitatively. So potential imitators of the Darbys, the pioneers in coke smelting, often found their natural skepticism reinforced by failures, and proclaimed that old ways were best. There was also prejudice on the part of customers against coke-made iron. The full breakthrough in metallurgy, especially for making machinery, came only with the development of a process for refining brittle cast iron to the more malleable wrought iron with the use of coal. This did not occur until 1785, just when Watt was perfecting his engine.

Although the supply of iron was thus assured and the mechanization of manufacturing and transport could begin, chemical ignorance was to make progress in ferrous metallurgy uncertain for many decades. Steel, which is chemically intermediate between cast and wrought iron, had no indus-

trial importance until the late 1860s (and even then industry ran afoul of complications due to impurities in ore).
The basic problem in steel stemmed from the difficulty of
controlling precisely the amount of carbon remaining in the
molten metal, since small differences in carbon content have
a great effect on physical properties. In more recent years,
the range of useful ferrous metals has been greatly extended
by the use of alloying materials.

Iron, coal, and steam found their largest applications in
transport and textiles, but they were also necessary to each
other. The supply of coal, much of it destined for smelting,
could be assured only if mining and transport equipment
made of metal was developed, eventually with steam trac-
tion. In turn, improvements in metallurgy were required for
the making of steam engines and the machinery they drove.
Finally, without the possibilities of mechanization provided
by steam power, it would have been impossible to develop
metallurgy on the scale required for efficiency in production. An industrial economy is not distinctive because men
use external sources of power or metal tools. It is the huge
quantity of power, fuel, and metal, and their cheapness,
that is essential.

One factor contributing greatly to the demand for coal
and iron, but even more perhaps to lowering their cost, was
the improvement in transport. England was, it is true, in a
fairly enviable position even before industrialization. Not
that her roads were anything but unspeakable. They were
worse than the French roads, which were far from good. But
the sea was never far in England, and the modest and
placid rivers were well suited to navigation. In order to provide adequate transportation for goods, it was merely necessary to complement coastal shipping by dredging some ports
and river channels and by digging relatively short canals.
The major effort was begun in the middle of the eighteenth
century.

One of the remarkable features of the canal boom was the
small role played by the government. Now that it is a com-
monplace to assign the state the task of building or supervis-

ing great projects of this sort, we can wonder at the way the English, with more modest financial and technical means, managed the job. To be sure, the richest men in the kingdom were not above getting involved. But the decisive factor was the mobilization of local capital on a wide scale. Here was something everyone could see and whose impact on the region or town was obvious. For the first time, an economic venture drew on the savings of thousands of passive partners: clergymen and widows as well as merchants and squires. It marked the expansion of the capital market, which had been limited to government and mercantile affairs, mainly in the City of London, into a national institution.

Roads were also built and improved, often by private initiative, as in the case of turnpikes, and elsewhere with local funds. This was far less successful than canal building. Roads needed upkeep, and could not compete with canals for carrying bulky goods. Later, the railroads took over most of the carrying trade, and road transport, though it increased and improved, did not really prosper until the internal-combustion engine arrived on the scene.

It was the railroad which put its stamp most firmly on the industrial age. Beginning with small mining roads in the 1820s, the new fad spread rapidly, until it became a mania in the 1840s. As in the case of canals, the government had a very small role to play and the private capital market a large one.

Despite the private nature of the railroad boom and because of the enthusiasm generated by this mode of transport, England very quickly acquired a fine network of lines, but the network was to pose problems in the long run. The railroads were well built, since capital was readily available and one might as well impress the stockholders with a solid job. But the system was very dense indeed, as neither promoters nor investors were inclined to be critical about the prospects for generating traffic. Furthermore, there was not the slightest hint of standardization, which would have been considered an affront to individual enterprise. Subsequent technical progress was often centered on trying to break speed records, because of the publicity value, while the problems of lowering the cost of moving freight, or avoiding reloading, or simplifying switching were of much less interest. However, the problems were for later. In the meantime, the railroad system was the pride of England and a fine source of export earnings when English engineers naturally specified English equipment for foreign railroads.

Industry in England needed a bread-and-butter product, one which would be easy to supply, lend itself to mechanization, and find a large and elastic market. This, in turn, would absorb the output of other industries, provide export earnings, give employment to many hands, and thus again stimulate business when wages were spent. As the reader hardly needs to be told, this industry was the manufacture of cotton cloth.

Cotton was not the most likely candidate. It was introduced into Europe at a time when the wool, silk, and linen industries had a long and noble record. For a long time it could not be used by itself, since only the East Indians seemed to have the nimble fingers needed to produce cotton thread strong enough for both warp and weft. But the fiber had wearing qualities that made it popular; it also took well to bright colors, so that the common people could shine in calico, as did the nobility in satins. Its lightness made it suitable for exports to warm climates, while the advantages, for hygiene and comfort, of having washable underclothing ensured a huge home market as well. Moreover, it was easy to expand the supply of cotton in the English colonies if not at home. Finally, although hard to spin by hand, cotton proved amenable to mechanization in a way that wool did not, as the prestige of hand-woven tweeds still attests.

The cotton trade began with imports and shifted to the home product when the wool men, feeling threatened, pressured Parliament into prohibiting Indian fabrics. As in the case of agriculture, it was not the leader whose technology changed, although the wool industry did eventually, if slowly, modernize. Just as the new agriculture flourished on previously marginal land, so mechanization took place chiefly in the upstart industry.

It is pretty clear that invention came in response to growth in the cotton industry, rather than the other way around. After all, a spinning machine is not the kind of thing one would invent in a spirit of disinterested scientific speculation. By 1750, a clear imbalance had arisen in cotton manufacture. The loom, though worked by hand and in cottages, had an appetite for thread that the "spinsters" could not satisfy even though the spinning wheel had replaced the distaff. The flying shuttle, breaking the limitation on cloth width imposed by the weaver's reach, made things worse.

The spinning bottleneck was the kind of problem for which there were several solutions, rather than a single one. Gadgets of varying value appeared and the two that came closest, the water frame and the jenny, were both developed around 1770. Each solved part of the problem. The former spun a strong but coarse thread, the latter a regular but weak one. Both machines could be used in conjunction, but they were later combined in the "mule" (1779).

All that was now required was to mount these gadgets in banks, connected by awkward shaft-and-belt arrangements to a water wheel or steam engine, and to put a roof over the whole business. Add hands to feed in cotton and to remove thread, and one had a cotton mill. Weaving continued to be done in sheds and cottages, the power loom taking a long time to displace the hand loom. When the former became efficient, Irish labor, fleeing the periodic famines, took over the hand looms and hung on despite ever-falling wages.

Cotton was important as an employer, as an export (and import) industry, and as a customer for machinery and chemicals. In Lancashire it was clearly dominant, and the Midlands relied on Lancashire business to sell their metal goods and potteries. But the changes in cotton were not unique. Elsewhere too, new firms were being started, factories built, power machinery installed, mass production methods introduced. Cotton was the leading sector, but it did not in any way "cause" development. If other activities had not responded eagerly to profit opportunities, the boom in cotton would simply have fizzled out when the extra demand it generated for machinery, food, transport, and housing drove up prices. No, the forces for development were there. In cotton they found a particularly apt material, one which confirmed the international orientation of the English economy that was to prove so fruitful. But even in 1851, at the height of the British cotton era, there were only 500,000 cotton workers out of 1.7 million engaged in large-scale industry and a total active population of some seven million. These figures should help establish some perspective, not only as regards the role of the cotton industry, but also in terms of the gradualness with which England became industrial. At the mid-century, there were still as many agricultural workers as there were men engaged in manufacturing and mining. And at the same time, the proportion of people living in large towns and cities first passed the one-half mark.

In all the cases of development we will study henceforth, and in countries attempting to modernize today, we find two principal actors whom we have so far not mentioned at all. They are the government and foreigners. As we have said, England's development was more private and more autonomous than any would ever be again. Yet it was not absolute in either respect. The positive cases of government intervention were relatively few, for example the right given railroads to force landowners to sell. Other acts stemmed from the new problems of an industrial society in matters of urban sanitation, work safety, and protection of women and children; they were only the first timid, and often bitterly fought, steps in the vast schemes of social welfare and public action that Europe would develop over the next century.

By far the most useful element of the government's action

was negative. As industry and trade expanded, a complex and archaic mass of regulations, prohibitions, statutes, and rules was swept away. To be sure, they had been honored in the breach rather than in the observance, and a few simple but enforced rules could make more difference to a businessman than much more stringent laws that were ignored. But the readiness of the government to adapt to new conditions proved a big help. The Reform Act of 1832, putting Parliament in the hands of the propertied classes generally rather than in those of landowners only, was a key step in the process. But the capstone of the edifice, the nearest to true laissez faire that the world has known before or since, was the freeing of foreign trade.

In 1846, the Corn Laws, limiting the import of grain, were repealed, and England entered on eighty-five years of virtually tariff-free trade, a unique experiment. From then on, the government was not totally out of the economic picture, but it limited its activity strictly to providing a favorable environment, where opportunity was tempered only by the need to maintain order (and eventually by a modicum of concern for the weak).

From foreigners, England took far less than she later paid back in financial and technical help. Perhaps this was only fair, since the competition provided by England would prove a strong hindrance, or at least a plausible excuse for failure, when industrialization began elsewhere, particularly in France. Yet England also drew on other countries, especially in the seventeenth century. Holland, which was ahead of Britain in many respects, provided capital and new techniques for wool finishing and land draining. From Flanders and France came refugees, fleeing the Spanish Inquisition and the dragoons of Louis XIV, respectively. These people were of more than average skill in a variety of trades, and their arrival provided benefits to early industrial expansion, especially since industrial technology was still far too empirical and informal to be diffused by means of books or training courses. When rapid industrialization began in England, the government tried to prevent the export of knowledge, but to no avail. Continental entrepreneurs were willing to pay any sum to find short cuts and catch up with the leader, and English craftsmen emigrated with their knowledge.

CHAPTER 10

The British Economy
in the
Nineteenth Century

The economic history of Britain from the mid-eighteenth century until the outbreak of World War I—a more natural end of the nineteenth century than the year 1900 itself—can be summarized with the familiar S-shaped learning curve. There was an acceleration, a period of rapid growth, and then a gradual slowdown. We have analyzed the elements of the development process in England that made possible the acceleration and the continuation of growth for a previously unheard-of length of time. In this chapter we shall look at the archetype of an industrial economy as it developed in England, consider the various subperiods in the general upward trend, and then analyze the retardation that set in late in the nineteenth century.

Change is more difficult to understand than a continuation of existing trends. Therefore, just as we devoted considerable attention to the important shift from an economy capable only of intermittent spurts of progress to one in which growth seemed to prepare the way for further growth, we shall be more concerned with the forces slowing down the "mature" British economy than with a description of the system in its heyday.

The cotton boom after 1760, interacting with the development of heavy industry and improved transport, propelled the British economy into a period of steady growth lasting over a century. There seemed to be no limit to expansion. Levels of activity, whether measured in numbers of people employed, power of machinery, or tons of materials used, that seemed staggering compared with the past, quickly faded into insignificance before new accomplishments.

Few bottlenecks arose. Labor was released by agriculture, even more by inefficient domestic industries as they were displaced, and by the increase of population. Raw materials came from underground sources that had hardly been tapped before, or from abroad. Larger markets were provided by increased incomes and new customers at home, and by prosperous communities blossoming in the empty temperate lands overseas. Capital was also plentiful, either because business profits were retained or because the new techniques saved capital at the same time as they required investment. Capital saving came from the efficiencies of transport and mass production, and from the division of labor between individuals and industries. Finally, progress in one industry provided not only profits for that industry, but also new opportunities and efficiency in others. We have already described the interactions between various parts of the iron-coal-steam complex, and their effect on textiles.

Only the food supply could not keep up, despite the considerable progress which, as we saw, took place in the period of development and later. England was too small, and the appetite of her people grew too quickly. But this proved no handicap so long as there were empty grain lands in the Americas, great sheep runs in Australia, and Danish or Dutch farmers willing to specialize in the requisites of a solid English breakfast: bacon, eggs, and butter.

The length and intensity of England's growth can per-

haps be explained by the extraordinary vigor and coherence
of the particular structure of production and institutions to
which she was committed. However, there was a price to pay
for having picked such a winner. When circumstances
changed, it was very difficult to stir up argument with the
system as it stood, and Britain then found the task of adapt-
ing herself to an economically changed world distasteful—
the more so, as she had been so good at coping with the first
stage of industrial development.

We have seen the essential features of Britain's industrial
structure. What were the main institutional tenets by which
she lived, indeed which she raised nearly to the status of
religious dogma?

One was full commitment to the market as the mechanism for allocating resources, establishing prices and incomes, and determining occupations. To be sure, businessmen often tried to combine in order to control a particular
market, while the government was forced to intervene to
mitigate the special hardships of the system or to deal with
minor items of clearly public business. Yet it was understood that the system functioned despite these imperfections, necessary or obstinate as they might be. An accepted
exception was monetary control, although the Bank of England was nominally a private organization.

Another tenet was private initiative and private property,
which put the full force of self-interest behind the market
mechanism, and which also made individuals bear the
brunt of that mechanism's outcome no matter how lavish or
harsh its decisions.

Finally, Britain was firmly committed to the principle of
international specialization, expressed by the theory of comparative advantage. The nation was not a natural economic
unit, which should strive to match its resources and needs.
Full specialization and efficiency, at least in many goods,
could be attained only by uniting the whole world. The
result would be to have each nation, like each region or individual, produce a small variety of goods while consuming
a much broader assortment. With mastery of the sea, with a

large empire, and in a world seemingly decided to relegate war to a secondary role in human affairs, there seemed to be little danger in this policy.

Although Britain occupied a particularly good position for international trade, we should not underestimate the magnitude of her commitment. When the Corn Laws were abolished, Britain accepted heavy specialization with its concomitants of dependence on others for necessities and of drastic transformation in the structure of production. The investment in comparative advantage paid handsomely. Englishmen "grew" more food by spinning cotton, manning ships, and balancing account books than they ever could have by tilling the soil. It is true that protection could have raised the income of farmers, but only at much greater cost to the rest of the population.

How did industrialization change the way Englishmen lived? For one thing, they lived increasingly in towns, and large towns at that. The rural England of independent yeomen, modest but secure in their picturesque cottages, had always been more myth than reality, but it was less and less relevant to the question of whether the standard of living of the masses was, or was not, improving.

This was, and has remained, the great controversy about the Industrial Revolution. Its notoriety comes not only from the inherent interest of the question, but also from the distinguished critics of early industrial society, especially Dickens in fiction and Marx and Engels in social thought. Actually, the problem of the poor had preoccupied the English before the industrial period. There were recurrent fears and rumors that an army of paupers would soon pose a threat to society, and various schemes were proposed for handling poor relief on the local level. These schemes combined charitable considerations with prudence and a strong sense of the moral and practical danger in simply doling out relief to anyone who needed it. It was felt that relief had to be meager and preferably tied in with work, so that the poor would have an incentive they otherwise lacked to find regular and respectable employment.

With industrialization, the misery moved into the towns, where it was visible and measurable to the people who wrote, read, and therefore made opinion. For this reason it was felt that industrialization created misery, when it is clear that most people went to the factories to escape worse conditions in rural industry or farming. There is evidence that workers in towns ate better than they had previously, but the very speed of industrialization made their living quarters in the new towns appallingly bad. Furthermore, the movements and changes accompanying the Industrial Revolution caused considerable social dislocation, so that misery was not relieved merely by very small improvements in income. Yet it must be noted that the period of worst conditions in London, the gin age, was before 1750. Finally, the effect of industrialization is overlaid, for the first period, with the consequences of more than twenty years of intermittent wars, which forced prices up much faster than wages rose.

It was natural that workers should unite to press their interests. As we saw earlier, the guilds were not the natural ancestors of labor unions, since they existed mainly to allow masters to control their employees and potential competitors. But the journeymen of medieval urban industries had also been organized in more or less secret societies—doubtless one of the features that encouraged entrepreneurs to look outside the towns for their labor. The associations of workers continued in the industrial age, especially after peace came in 1815. But the market-oriented temper of the times, so unfavorable to legislation of a charitable nature, was equally suspicious of combinations that might seek to influence the market decision in the direction of greater returns to labor. The right to associate was not granted workers in England until 1825, and then was strongly hedged with restrictions, particularly against the right to strike.

Yet this period was one rich in social experiments, combining the principles of the French Revolution with a good dose of romanticism, in keeping with the current literary fashion. These experiments, Robert Owen's for example, alternated between trying to humanize and discipline the industrial explosion on the one hand and denouncing it on the other.

Of more immediate consequence were the craft unions, which embarked on a limited and pragmatic program of action after the failure of the first ambitious industrial unions under the Chartist movement. Especially after 1850, they were concerned with the welfare of well-defined groups of industrial workers, such as miners or dockers, and were mutual-aid or insurance societies as much as collective bargaining organizations. It was not until 1890 that a mass labor movement would again exert any influence in Britain. Meanwhile, the craft union, with its concern for specific material ends rather than generalized action or class struggle and with its appeal to the aristocracy of labor, would profoundly mark the American labor movement.

Despite the continued presence of poverty and its aggravation in certain cases where the winds of change blew most harshly, the dominant social feature of industrial England was the rise of the middle classes: in numbers, in wealth, and in power. They were the great beneficiaries of the new abundance of consumer goods, of higher incomes, and of the many opportunities for profitable ventures. Victorian England, particularly in its moral and aesthetic standards, was very much their age.

The social order, of which the middle class now formed the central element, was neither truly fluid nor highly rigid. There were rather clear distinctions between the upper classes, the lower classes, and a well-defined intermediate group. But the boundaries were not sharp, and, more importantly, they could be crossed. It might take a generation before the workman who became a shopkeeper or an independent entrepreneur would be thought of as middle class, or before the manufacturer could lay claim to the title of "gentleman." Yet the requisites could be bought with money and time. Schooling for one's children and the purchase of land generally did the trick.

Above all, few people challenged the existing social order. They might try to improve the material lot of their family or group and aim at a higher social position for their descendants, but they accepted inequalities of wealth and position, and in particular did not envisage leveling them through the political system, as the French often sought to do.

Let us now examine the rhythm of British economic growth, and in particular the fluctuations around the underlying trend of steady growth followed by gradual retardation. Following W. W. Rostow, we can distinguish two kinds of periods. In the first, generally thought of as booms, prices tended to rise, even though the nineteenth century was unique in economic history in the limited extent of its inflations. In between these periods, and also lasting roughly twenty-five years, were so-called depressions, marked by a general tendency to falling prices. The inflationary periods were from 1780 to the end of the war in 1815, from the crisis of 1848 to that of 1873, and from the recovery of 1896 to the outbreak of World War I. This leaves two long deflationary phases, from 1815 to 1848 and from 1873 to 1896. The latter of these has been called the Great Depression, although we in America reserve that name for the unpleasantness of the 1930s.

It is important to look more closely at the two kinds of phases and to see whether the usual labels are appropriate. In the so-called booms, agricultural prices tended to go up more than industrial. This should have hurt manufacturers, but they found that foreign suppliers of foodstuffs to Britain were so prosperous that they bought large quantities of goods. So profits were high, while wages went up in money terms more than in purchasing power. Farmers did relatively well, and somehow their voices, with those of businessmen, were louder than those of workers. To be sure, since business was good, jobs were at least relatively plentiful even if real wage rates did not rise much.

One more phenomenon needs to be noted. Since foreign producers were doing particularly well, there was an incentive for British investors to take their capital out of the country. Perhaps this contributed to taking the bloom off the domestic scene, with productivity not growing very fast despite the satisfaction of businessmen.

Of course, this schematic representation neglects the features particular to each separate period. For example, in the Napoleonic period inflation was pushed by war, whereas the boom of the 1850s was fed by gold discoveries in California and South Africa, and that of the end of the century by the Klondike. Capital exports did not play an important part in the first period, while English agriculture was too far gone to profit by the last inflationary phase just prior to World War I. Nonetheless, the general pattern holds.

In contrast, we have to look more carefully at the gloomy reports describing the state of the economy in the so-called depressed periods. Profits do seem to have been lower and unemployment higher, although we cannot really measure either accurately. But wages were rising, in terms of the goods they would buy, while the supply of savings, though it was reduced by lower profits, at least was made available to home investors. This was a time for those investments which are not spectacular, not born of euphoric prospects, but rather are forced by the need to lower costs and to meet stiff competition. Yet this kind of investment generates real, and cumulatively important, gains in productivity that eventually show up in higher incomes.

It is true that agriculture failed to share in the general advance. After the high prices of the Napoleonic Wars, when any land could yield a profit if planted to grain, the awakening was rude. Enclosure then bore its full fruits, in the sense that the greater efficiency it made possible was enforced by a hard market. On the other hand, the period following the removal of import restrictions on grain, after the crisis of 1846–1848, did not bear out the fears of those who thought free trade would ruin the English farmer. In fact, this was the so-called period of "high farming," when machinery and chemical fertilizers were introduced and the productive mixed agriculture of the past century was thus further developed. The removal of protection provided the stick, and continuing high prices the carrot.

Perhaps it was unfortunate for England that her agriculture was not forced to make a more drastic adjustment to free trade. For in the long run, England could not remain a supplier of grain and beef cattle. This became manifest after 1873, when great ships of iron and steam began to dump the harvests of the American plains on European shores at unheard-of low prices. Denmark and Holland were ready, but England and France were not. As we shall see, the French restored the tariff walls, but England was too far committed to a large industrial population, requiring abundant and cheap food. Her agriculture stagnated and dwindled, never to revive except as a near-vestigial sector carried along by government subsidies.

Why did English farmers not shift from grain and beef, in which they could not compete, to the specialty products— fruit, dairy, poultry, vegetables—with which English housewives would assure the prosperity of other European farmers? Not for the last time in this book, we are here asking about the failure of an economy or an industry to develop while others were proving it could be done. Perhaps we can postpone the various explanations until we consider the English slowdown as a whole, although it was nowhere nearly so drastic as in agriculture. For the time being, we can justly suspect that the English farmer may simply have been afflicted with the "Arkansas Traveler" syndrome: he would not fix his roof when it was raining, and the roof did not leak any other time!

There is no reason why the economic record of a country, say its rate of growth of income per capita, should have to be compared with that of other countries. Yet economic races existed long before the ideological dispute between East and West made battle slogans out of goulash and the two-car garage. The late nineteenth century, with its heightened international rivalries and imperial expansions, was just as concerned with relative economic performance. To those who could look at trends rather than at absolute levels, it was clear that Britain, though still a leader in many respects, was not running as fast as others. Although part of this slowing down was illusory, or at least merely relative to the dramatic pace set by Germany and by the young giant in North America, the statistical evidence does suggest some absolute retardation as well. Britain did not stop growing; but the rate of growth decreased.

It is ironic that the British should have failed to learn from the Darwinian doctrine of evolution that organisms that adapt too successfully to one set of conditions are handicapped when those conditions change. We have seen how fully British society and economic patterns were shaped by her industrialization or were at least compatible with it. Now new forces were appearing, and Britain was hampered by this closely integrated structure and, it must be said, by the smugness that so neat a system had engendered. The most important changes were in the structure of world production and in the nature of technology.

For a long time, Britain had been the "workshop of the world." She supplied the bulk of the industrial goods, chiefly textiles, railroad equipment, and steam-run machinery for a world beginning to add consumer-good manufactures to a largely agrarian structure. The development of other economies, especially in the temperate lands overseas, meant, for a time, increased markets for these British goods. But others also learned how to make cotton textiles, how to smelt iron, and even how to make machinery. Some of the learners remained behind Britain in their efficiency and scale, and could at best hope to capture their own domestic market. France, Italy, Austria-Hungary, and Russia were examples; but others had considerable advantages in natu-

ral resources and showed the entrepreneurial qualities
needed for rapid development. The United States was one,
but Germany, and later Japan, proved even more troublesome, since they competed with the British in export
markets as well as at home.

Of equal importance to the future of manufacturing was
the rise of a new family of industries. In a world of change,
it is normal that demand should shift from one set of products to another, but the new "leading sectors," to use the
fashionable term, represented more than just a different set
of goods. We have noted the empirical character of technical progress in textiles and iron. Chemicals, electrical equipment, light metals, synthetics, and vehicles would rely on a
very different source of technical progress, born of science.
The economic consequence of this was to require systematic
expenditure on expensive and uncertain research and development, demanding new entrepreneurial qualities of risk
taking and different managerial attitudes. Another require-
ment would be for a different kind of "human" capital, as
embodied in highly trained technical and scientific personnel. Literacy, factory discipline, and commercial and craft
skills, though still relevant, were no longer of primary importance.

It was particularly appropriate for Britain to take the
lead in developing the new style of industry. She had the
advantage of a strong industrial tradition, abundant capital, a large middle class, and a tradition of pragmatic adaptation to reality rather than refuge in myth and doctrine.
Moreover, there was no country that depended so much on
staying ahead technically as this small, highly populated island with its modest natural resources. The whole basis of
English prosperity was to add much value, in terms of labor,
capital, and skill, to raw materials, often imported, and to
sell the embodied resources of England abroad to those who
could not provide them so efficiently. Nonetheless, and despite all kinds of qualifications and numerous British successes, we can fairly return a rather harsh verdict. The main
reason for the slowdown of Britain was failure to take full

advantage of the new opportunities, and, instead, her continued reliance on traditional goods and methods with steadily diminishing market potential.

In certain ways, the British were handicapped by institutions increasingly inappropriate to new conditions. This was true, for example, of the typical industrial firm, managed by the owner and his family and adhering to one specific pattern of business. More complex techniques and new products required a massive effort for working out problems at all stages of processing, from raw material through to selling the finished product and showing the user how to make the most of its advantages. Later we shall see how this operated in the great German firms.

However, many British firms not only failed to adapt to new requirements, but also lost the aggressiveness of earlier years. The descendants of the industrial pioneers were far less eager to carry on with the same energy as the founders. Born to wealth, they tended to view their mission as that of consolidating the social position of the family. Although they seldom gave up the business entirely, the office week was often badly trimmed at both ends. When the firm owner was not playing the gentleman farmer, he was frequently involved in public business, whether in Parliament or in some of the many benevolent or scientific associations so typical of Britain. The men left in effective charge of the business appear to have been concerned more often with keeping things going than with exploring fully any new opportunities for profit. Britain, of course, had no monopoly on the phenomenon of declining economic dynasties. In France and New England too, the aggressive generations were often succeeded by playboys, scholars, philanthropists, or diplomats. And the best German literary account is Thomas Mann's saga of the *Buddenbrooks,* merchants of Lübeck.

The education problem played an important role. The British had benefited earlier, as we have seen, from the presence of educated younger sons of the upper classes, while popular schooling, though not organized on a massive public scale, had contributed a literate and often skilled labor force. But technical, not to say managerial, training was badly slighted. Whether the fault lay in the schools or lack of them, or in industrialists who had no use for experts, it is hard to say. Undoubtedly, the tradition of amateurism, relying on the common sense of a man with no specialized training to cloud his mind, exercised a great fascination. To the extent that social forces promoted the recruitment of managers from among the wellborn, they reinforced the predominance of men with a liberal rather than a technical background.

Nevertheless, all this is insufficient to explain the failure of British firms to play a greater role in new industries and improved techniques. We can understand the conservatism of established firms. But why were they challenged so little, except by foreigners? Why did not new enterprises spring up, in new industries and old, to take advantage of the leisurely pace of competition and quicken it in the process? In no country was it so easy for new firms to get a foothold, in the sense that law and custom placed limitations on agreements between firms to monopolize markets. The mechanism of change was familiar to England: the cotton industry had grown even though there was great resistance to mechanization in wool; and eastern England had transformed its agriculture despite the difficulties in changing techniques on the clay lands of the West. The British simply did not grab the opportunity to build up giant, innovative industries. On the contrary, the followers, Germany and, in particular, the United States took the lead in developing new techniques. Perhaps they felt that the British lead in traditional lines was too great and that England had to be outflanked. But as early as the 1850s, the Americans were ahead in agricultural machinery and in operating their mechanical industries on the basis of interchangeable parts. Somewhat later, the Germans made great strides in chemical and steel production, both British-born industries. Finally, both competitors showed the way in electricity, again despite the prominence of British scientists in discovering its laws.

Let us consider for a moment the case of chemicals and

that of steel, for they show the weakness of some traditional explanations, focusing on deficiency in demand for the goods involved or on lack of the right resources for their production. England was the unchallenged leader in heavy chemicals, mainly soda ash for textiles, soap, and glass, and sulfuric acid for various uses. Her prominence in textiles also influenced her concern for dyestuffs, and a young chemical student made the first synthetic dye in London in 1856. Yet by 1880, when England was still synonymous with textiles and industry in general, chemical production had undergone a crisis. A new process for soda, which Britain did not adopt, was making her established producers lose money, while the textile industry was buying great amounts of synthetic dyestuffs from Germany and even little Switzerland. What had happened? Very little, and that was precisely the problem. Existing firms clung to tried-and-true techniques, and no new ones sprang up to do business in the new way, with the laboratory calling the tune.

Steel was less clear-cut, though again England lost a leading position. The first large-scale steel process was developed by Bessemer in 1856, while another Englishman, Sidney Gilchrist Thomas, solved the challenging problem of making steel when the ore contained phosphorus. Yet his process, which could use almost any ore, was only slowly adopted in England, while Continental manufacturers, in the Ruhr especially, were far more eager. People in Britain objected that the new steel was "less good," or the investments were "too costly," or the new process was "not reliable." Eventually, of course, Britain went along, and there were never shortages of steel, but the delay and unwillingness to change are symptomatic. There are other examples as well, particularly in coking, where England failed to install new ovens that would capture the valuable by-products, and also in electricity and, surprisingly, even in textiles.

One should not exaggerate. There *was* technical progress in England. However, it tended to consist of varied improvements trying to squeeze every bit of possible productivity from existing methods. English practices were invariably the best-developed examples of their kind, but their kind was too often obsolete. Clearly there was an unwillingness to start over, to scrap everything and begin with a fresh sheet of paper and with a study of the basic principles. That was somehow too professional. Perhaps it is true that new ventures could not get easy access to funds, while the firms with plenty of cash had no special interest in using it to finance uncertain innovation. Yet the reluctance of savers to entrust their funds to the more venturesome investors, if that was the problem, also contrasts with the spirit of the Industrial Revolution, in which men somehow found, locally and with little recourse to banks, the capital needed to get going. True, the sums were now somewhat greater, but so was the wealth of the country.

Yet we must not end the story of Britain in the nineteenth century on this negative note. For it would give entirely the wrong impression of the vitality of economic life in Britain in the late Victorian and the Edwardian periods. England was a bustling land, full of intense productive activity, and London was the unchallenged financial and commercial center of the world. Even when trade took place between two non-British traders and the goods never came within 5,000 miles of London, there was a good chance that the transaction would add to the total of Britain's "exports," and income. The ship that carried the goods would be English or at least would be insured and chartered through London. The goods, too, were often insured in London, where the banking aspects of the trade also were easily handled, as all serious international traders kept accounts there. It was in London that the market for various currencies and gold was centered, there or in Liverpool that most commodity prices were determined. A large part of London depended somehow or other on foreign trade for its livelihood, while the payments of foreigners for these services allowed Britain to enjoy considerable extra imports or to increase her financial holdings abroad. In the long run, the growing prosperity of other nations would pose grave problems to Britain's industry, but for the time being it only added to the volume of business transacted in the City and along the docks.

Behind the glittering facade of long-distance trade and high finance, a whole nation worked and lived in a new world, rapid in its pace, harsh in its treatment of tradition, capable of the heights of grandeur and the depths of vulgarity. Everything that men identified with industry and with a world-wide economy was typified by Britain: the cosmopolitan foodstuffs of the "English" diet, the dingy factories and row houses, the great bridges and tunnels, the bourgeois houses, ornate and stuffy, but better heated and more comfortable than any palace of previous times—all this was England. Older stereotypes of great country houses, thatched cottages, and shocking exploitation of child labor were still alive, but fading in significance. The leveling force of industrial progress was replacing them with more uniform and less picturesque images. If it lacked grandeur or pathos, the industrial civilization at least spared more and more people the extremes of want and suffering. Despite the doctrine of laissez faire and the fear that charity softened the will to work, more goods were in fact available. Gradually, everyone received at least some share of the increase, in higher wages or, eventually, in some form of social welfare help.

CHAPTER 11

France and the
Hesitations
of Development

In our discussion of the competitors who grew up in the second half of the nineteenth century to challenge England's dominance in industry and trade, France has been conspicuous by her absence. Yet this country, the most populated in Western Europe until the second half of the century, was the first, if we except Belgium, to follow the British lead in beginning the process of development. The modesty and gradualness of industrialization in France form a striking contrast to the pioneering vigor of England, the sweep of American expansion, the relentless pace at which Germany caught up with the leader. However, French economic history can also be considered in comparison with other countries of Europe, particularly to the south and east, and this comparison makes it clear that there was modernization and development. The qualities of balance and moderation—*mesure* in French—have been much prized in French culture, and they apply equally to her reaction to the great force of economic growth introduced by England's example.

Whether one concludes that French development was slow or rapid, there is no question that the country was less sharply changed by industrialization than most others. On the other hand, it was not torn, as some were, by failure to come to terms with the new phenomena. I would suggest that the concern for continuity in the social and cultural spheres is basic to an understanding of the special character of France's story. On the other hand, that story can perhaps cast light on some basic problems of development and particularly on the respective roles of revolution and evolution, of discontinuity and gradualness, in the process.

We saw earlier that the beginnings of development were retarded in France by social rigidity and crisis-ridden public finances. The political outcome of this combination, the Revolution and the imperial reaction, further put off any widespread beginnings of modern growth. There were, to be sure, important changes in the social structure and in the institutional framework of economic activity, as well as various tangible changes in the productive apparatus. But the effects of new laws and changed distribution of property were neither immediate nor unambiguously favorable to development, while many of the new industrial ventures did not outlive the war economy in which they had been started. In any case, the wars themselves, so costly in men, treasure, and social energies, sharply limited the prospects for economic development.

What is more surprising is the absence of a strong positive reaction after peace and social stability had returned, namely in the period of the Restoration and the July Monarchy (1815–1848). France and Europe were at peace. There were few great political causes to engage the energies of men or to cloud economic prospects.[2] The major legal and social

2 A good example of the perspective afforded by economic history is the realization that great dates of French history, such as 1830 and, later, 1870, were hardly more than political tempests in a Parisian teapot. Their effects on social and economic conditions throughout France were in fact slight.

reforms of the Revolution were maintained, and indeed scarcely challenged. For the last eighteen years of the period, the crown sat on the head of a bourgeois monarch, and his ministers openly based their power on the financial leaders in Paris. There was a backlog of example and technique that had been built up across the Channel, while the government was willing to protect the French economy from too sudden exposure to the aggressive blast of English competition—perhaps too willing. While protection could give shelter to fragile starts, it also tended to defer change or at least to remove the necessary urgency from the enterprise of development. Nowhere is the slow pace of change more evident than in the construction of railroads. While England, Belgium, and even splintered Germany were madly caught up in the fashion of the day, the French engaged in long discussions and planning procedures on the best way to deal with such a major innovation. The result was to delay construction of all but a few lines until the 1850s.

As in 1789, it was an economic crisis that precipitated the revolution of 1848. However, this was a more "economic" event than the overthrow of the *ancien régime* had been, marked as it was by the first political expression of socialist thought. But the reformist agitation was quickly repressed, and had few immediate economic consequences. An authoritarian and politically conservative regime took over, but one more concerned with economic growth or at least more receptive to it. The Second Empire was a period of sustained growth, rapid by the standards of nineteenth-century France, although the pace slackened distinctly in the decade of the 1860s. Even the War of 1870, traumatic as its political implications may have been, apparently had little effect on the economic development of France. Nevertheless, the end of the 1870s inaugurated another of these strangely stagnant periods in France, strange in that external conditions seemed conducive to better performance.

Let us consider for a moment the implications of the last statement. It is not difficult to find reasons for slow French growth, say between 1875–1879 and 1896, and we shall soon pass to a discussion of explanations for retardation. But this method is misleading, in that it neglects the "why" and focuses only on the "how." As a result, one begins with the fact of slow growth, enumerates the possible causes, and then describes the period in terms of these causes, neglecting other aspects that were also present and should have contributed to a more favorable economic picture. In the present case, for example, peace again prevailed in Europe, a reasonable political consensus was being elaborated in republican France, and plentiful technical opportunities were open to French enterprise, both in established sectors where France still had not gone very far and in the new industries and techniques of which we spoke in the last chapter. Even the national humiliation of 1870 should have acted as a spur to growth, since it was clearly recognized that national power depended on a modern economy, that an army really did "march on its stomach," as Napoleon had said.[3]

After 1896 and down to World War I, which would so sorely try France, the pace of progress definitely accelerated, although it still retained characteristic French *mesure*. The numerical results were good chiefly by comparison with the past, while remaining modest on an international scale. Nor can one speak of any real transformation of the French economy. It was qualitatively very much unchanged, only there was rather more of everything, particularly in the recently developed branches of industry. Indeed, the French were so conditioned to their own inferiority in textiles, iron and steel, and organic chemicals that they tended to overlook quite respectable and promising positions in aluminum, automobiles, industrial gases, and other industrial fledglings.

Thus, our periodization of the nineteenth century has been the same for France as for England. Only in the present case, the alternating periods, leaving aside the Revolu-

[3] Consider the striking contrast with Denmark. The Danes, too, had lost a war and some provinces to Prussia, but they were spurred to spectacular development, particularly in agriculture. On the basis of rural education, research, and rational specialization, they managed to achieve efficiency within the framework of the small family farm.

tion and the Napoleonic Wars, really do represent changes in the rhythm of growth. In England, by contrast, we suggested that the "booms" were perhaps less rosy than they seemed, and the "depressions" far from stagnant. The quantitative evidence for France is not very good, but it clearly shows a pattern of real alternation in rates of growth. Why was the French economy so much more sensitive, apparently, to movements in world prices, bearing in mind that the role of foreign trade was far more limited in France than in Britain?

Three reasons suggest themselves. The first relates to the continuing importance of agriculture in France, particularly of the rural sector as an industrial market. Precisely because French industry did not rely on exports to any extent, its prosperity depended closely on agricultural incomes and therefore on agricultural prices. And as we have seen, these tended to fluctuate more strongly than industrial prices, so that the deflationary periods depressed the agricultural sector sharply—and consequently hurt French industrial prosperity.

The second reason stems from the gradual nature of French industrialization. There were really no industrial booms in France, no massive movements into one industry or group of activities in response to new markets or techniques, similar to the cotton or railroad eras in England. Yet such booms, in which increasing returns to scale and various cumulative effects of growth operate on a substantial scale in a self-reinforcing way are particularly resistant to cyclical disturbances. They have their own dynamics and are little affected by general deflation or bad crops. In turn, an economy enjoying such a boom has forces for counteracting crises and depressions, and has more chances of absorbing them without seriously interrupting its growth. There were no such coattails to which the French economy could cling in harder times.

Finally, it is a fundamental aspect of development that necessary changes are eased by prosperity, whereas uncertainty or crisis increase the costs of moving, changing occu-

pation, or undertaking some unfamiliar kind of enterprise.
And France appears to have been particularly sensitive to
the social cost of development, in terms of the transformations it imposed. When business was buoyant, even if price
rises put pressure on the standard of living, the costs seemed
bearable, but when pessimism reigned, there was general
unwillingness to change, and this refusal to "transform" the
economy interfered with growth. Of course, the effects were
cumulative in both cases, since slow growth made depressions more severe, and strengthened the reluctance to leave
familiar ways. It required a fundamental change in the at-
mosphere and in price trends to start a cumulative process
of confidence, mobility, innovation, growth, and greater
confidence. For this reason, alternating periods of slow and
relatively rapid growth are rather long.

   Several aspects of the French economy stand out as distinctive, and we shall describe some of them before suggesting an explanation of the factors common to all of them.
Our discussion will touch on population change, the agricultural system, the family firm, the role of foreign trade,
and spatial mobility.[4]
   France's failure to partake of the demographic explosion
that coincided with industrialization in Europe is perhaps
the most strikingly original facet of her economic history.
Demographic patterns have causes deeply entwined with the
social and cultural fabric of the society and with its economic life. In return, they affect every dimension of a community, from its attitudes and institutions to the level of
demand and the need for social investments. France shared
in the general nineteenth century fall in death rates, though
she was not a leader in reducing mortality. But while other
countries experienced prolonged periods of high birth rates,
or even a probable temporary rise in the case of England,

   [4] In the interests of brevity and sharpness, we shall again be forced to
overseparate and to overdraw, and the reader is referred back to the
introductory *caveat* regarding the perils of surveys.

this bulge was almost nonexistent in France. From 1800 to 1850, her population grew rather slowly (but it did grow), from about 27 million to 36½ million, which still made France larger than Germany and two thirds again as populous as the United Kingdom. But from then on and until World War II, birth rates in France were so low that they contributed nothing to any further increase in population. With continuing decreases in mortality rates, the effect mainly of medical improvements and better sanitation, the population inched up to some 41½ million at the outbreak of World War I. The war and the depression of the 1930s reduced this to something under the 40 million Frenchmen into whom France was supposed to be divided. Table 1 gives a few comparative figures for other European countries. The contrast with France is obvious.

TABLE 1   *Population of European Countries (in millions)*

	1850	1910	1940
United Kingdom	22.3	42.1	48.2
Germany	31.7	58.5	69.8
Italy	23.9	36.2	43.8

It is possible to explain the retardation of the French economy by the demographic factor, although awkward details persist, such as the poor performance in the early nineteenth century and the more rapid growth following the end of even slow demographic increase after 1850. But a more fundamental objection is that we can find no justification for assigning the role of cause to population and of effect to economic growth. We could just as easily put things the other way around: because there was not much increase in income, the French chose, in some imperfectly understood way, to limit the size of their families. In fact, of course, population and economic growth interact, and we can at least say that small families and a stable population contributed to the rigidities that marked the French economy, and thus to sluggish growth. Demographic stagnation made it possible for children to follow in the footsteps of their parents, limited the demand for goods and for certain investments, and emphasized the political role and economic responsibilities of the elderly, who were relatively numerous.

The relation between family size and occupational continuity was of special importance in farming. French agriculture did not go through the changes characteristic of the sector in England, or rather experienced them only timidly and over a limited area. The Revolution accelerated and completed a process of agrarian change that had been under way for some time and which resulted in France's becoming a land of peasant proprietors. But only in the rich plains of the north and around Paris did large-scale farms grow up, some owner-worked, many farmed out by town-dwelling owners to the same kind of substantial tenants who applied innovations in Norfolk and Essex. Elsewhere small farms continued to predominate, as did owner occupancy.

The drawbacks of small farms and inadequate capital were aggravated by the effects of equal inheritance, resulting in parcelization of land often to the point of absurdity. Yet the legal system was not alone to blame, for it was possible to consolidate holdings by exchange—possible in the abstract, but not in French practice. The reason has to do with the weak commitment of the French peasant to the market. Although he usually sold at least some part of what he grew or raised, the primary purpose of his activity was to feed himself and his family. A man needed his own wheat field, his own pasture and fruit trees, and of course his own small vineyard. This outlook encouraged diversity of production and therefore of soils. Besides, agreement on the equivalence between two parcels of land was difficult to obtain in a society prizing land above all else, and cash mainly for the land it would buy. Finally, the peasant was usually poor, and felt he could not afford to risk everything on one crop, which might, after all, fail.

Being inefficient as a producer, the farmer, though thrifty, could seldom mobilize enough capital to modernize his

methods. But there were other reasons for technical backwardness. Small parcels of land would not benefit from
mechanization. Nor could a poor man give up the twenty
bushels an acre he was fairly sure of for the possible thirty-
five to forty he was told English farmers considered normal.
More important, even, than the lack of capital goods was
the inadequate investment in learning, especially technical
and applied education for agriculture. Finally, the peasant
had a deep suspicion of outsiders—of the city people represented by the tax collector, the slick seller of dubious miracle fertilizers, and the grasping monopolist who bought his
produce. The government was prepared to do much for the
peasant, but it would not take the steps necessary to break
his isolation, to modernize his outlook and methods, and to
protect him from sickness and fraud so he could be free to
take more constructive risks. Advice was plentiful, but no
one offered to share the risks of change. So the French peasant preferred to produce as he had done, to use any cash he
could patiently accumulate for buying an extra little patch
of field, and to hope he would not have too many children,
so that the farm would not be further split up.

One minor mystery concerns the role of large landowners,
particularly aristocrats. When the political power of the
English nobility declined, in the seventeenth and eighteenth centuries under the Whigs and again after the Reform of 1832, they often retired to their estates and devoted
their energies to improvements in farming and stockbreeding
and to laying out their beautiful parks and gardens. We
have picturesque literary examples of these men, from
Fielding's Squire Western to P. G. Wodehouse's Lord Ems-
worth. In France, however, the "internal emigration" of the
aristocracy after 1830 produced no comparable interest in
agricultural techniques. While the actual holdings of this
class were proportionately less in France than in England, it
retained enough local power and prestige to have swayed
rural fashions toward greater concern with agricultural
progress, as its role in lobbying organizations proves.

All was not dark, it is true. There was the North and the

Beauce, as productive as any regions in Europe, and there were highly developed specialty productions, from the wines of Burgundy and Bordeaux to the fruit of the South and the cheeses of so many provinces. Though irregular in quality and subject to attacks by pests, French agricultural produce had a taste only enhanced by the culinary tradition it made possible. But the cost was enormous. Not only did farmers produce at low efficiency, but the archaic structure of agriculture was mirrored and complemented by an equally backward distribution network, employing a vast number of people of low productivity.

The industrial analogue of the independent farm was the family firm. Until the end of the nineteenth century most industrial enterprises in Europe were owned by one man or by a few partners. The large corporation, where many owners gave up any real managerial control in exchange for the advantages of limited liability, played an increasing but still minor role. Yet nowhere was the firm so closely identified with the owner, and especially with the succeeding generations of his family, as in France. In the short run the family was entirely at the service of the business, whose continued profitable existence was, in turn, the guarantor of the family's continued place in the sun.

There were important consequences of the close ties between family and firm, which were largely inimical to rapid growth. For one thing, the fortunes of the firm depended on the supply of competent managers, and recruitment was in principle limited to descendants. As we have seen for the English firm, this reservoir might not provide a sufficient supply, although there was perhaps less disinterest on the part of later-generation owners than we have noted for the English. In addition, French firms recruited managers by the process of absorbing them into the family, usually as sons-in-law who added the family name to their own. Nonetheless, the necessity of maintaining the close identification between family and firm posed problems. A man's position in the latter depended on his seniority rather than on his aptitude for business, while family feuds could lead to a breakdown of communication in the company.

The general hostility to outsiders went beyond unwilling-ness to entrust the management of the firm to one of them. This hostility extended to bankers, the government, techni-cal experts, and even customers! All were potential sources of enforced change or loss of control. The banker generally required much information before making a loan, particu-larly for a long period, and he might demand a supervisory role. The government threatened to permit foreign compe-tition, and sent tax collectors to inspect the books as well as exact payment. The engineer felt he must justify his exist-ence and salary by continually suggesting new ways to spend money. Finally, the fickle customer threatened to insult the pride of the family by preferring some cheap novelty to the traditional product that had made the firm more than just a way of making money. As a sociologist has said, the bour-geois family of France espoused the aristocratic values of quality and uniqueness.

Most important, perhaps, the connection between the en-terprise and the family made bankruptcy, or even takeover by another firm, the catastrophe to be avoided at all costs. With this in mind, it is easy to understand the reluctance to take risks, and in particular to tie up funds in an uncertain enterprise with a payout far in the future. Who knew what depressions might come in the meantime? We must avoid judging the French firm by a set of objectives, such as maxi-mum sales or profits, which they did not share. In particu-lar, they found it preferable to avoid lowering prices to the point of driving less efficient competitors out of business, since the continued existence of this buffer meant reasona-ble profits for the better firms without the need to expand rapidly or to cut costs.

The above picture is overdrawn, or rather it omits impor-tant elements. These French entrepreneurs had great devo-tion to their firm, and were often technically brilliant as well as managerially capable. They were able to achieve

their objectives in many cases, and especially to survive difficult times. Furthermore, the type of limited competition
and hesitant investment policies characteristic of France
made crises less sharp, even though they also slowed the pace
of growth. The most serious consequence seems to have been
a bias against complex technical innovation requiring considerable investment and giving more of a voice in the firm
to young upstarts from engineering schools, with their fancy
jargon. In turn, men with ideas could seldom find backing
from existing firms, and had to face all the difficulties of
starting from scratch with limited financial means. In the
long run, the career choices of able young men were biased
against applied science and against industry.

The desire to protect established positions, even at the
cost of abandoning the possibility of great improvement,
was an important aspect of the low mobility of the French.
As we have seen, farmers hesitated to exchange parcels of
land, and entrepreneurs to change their products and techniques. But the phenomenon was more general. In no country of Europe was urbanization more gradual, and nowhere
were people more reluctant to migrate, either out of the
country or to another region. Yet France would probably
have gained at least from greater regional mobility. For the
best agricultural regions were often equally well suited to
industrial development, while less-favored areas had neither. Thus labor was scarce in the one and unable to find
productive employment in the other. Yet people would not
move from the Massif Central to the North or from Brit-
anny to Lorraine. When they did move, it was to Paris,
where there were (and are) established colonies of Breton
maids and bartenders, and of postmen from the Southwest.
Industry had to pry people from the farms in areas where
agricultural labor was not overabundant, or to import foreign workers. Even in the 1960s, the coal miners of Decaze-
ville, in the Massif Central, resisted transfer to more productive mines because they would have to abandon the
town cemetery!

Hesitant development was surprisingly feasible in France,

probably because there was a fairly strong social consensus against rocking the boat in the name of modernization. Yet one force did threaten the consensus from outside, and it took the form of international economic competition. For this reason, virtually all French industrialists and farmers were united on the virtues of protection. The few who were not and who saw a future in exporting fought a losing battle, especially after the fall of Napoleon III, himself a free trader. The export-minded Alsatian industrialists moved or became German, while the winegrowers had to fight the terrible blight of phylloxera, and could not challenge the protectionist chorus. So the bold liberalization of trade introduced by the 1860 treaty with Britain was slowly eroded, until full protection, or almost full, was reestablished in 1892. Yet it was a fallaciously cozy solution for the French economy. While giving up many of the benefits of specialization, French producers often found that the advantages they received from protection were entirely offset by higher costs of production because of the protection given others. To protect everyone meant, in essence, to protect no one. The major consequence of the policy was to entrench in France the principle that government was the natural source of relief from economic woes, an idea that was pernicious in its principle as well as ineffectual in its results.

Other factors have been advanced to explain the slowness of French economic growth, particularly the modest resources of the country in coal and certain other natural resources, and the difficulties in linking various regions by an efficient transport system. I do not think that these explanations are very helpful, although of course more coal would have been welcome, and of course France would have benefited from having the Loire and the Rhone be placid and navigable rivers. But coal can be imported, while it was in fact discouraged from entering by a tariff; canals can replace rivers, and railroads replace water transport, whereas France tended to lag in developing both.

However, the mere listing of problems and factors of retardation is insufficient, the more so as they reinforced each other. Can we identify a common force in the various factors, a more basic cause that manifested itself in demography, agriculture, commercial policy, and other factors?

I would suggest that France was marked by very strong social conservatism. More than in any other nation that has gone through the process of development, perhaps excepting Japan, the French had an acute awareness of the changes that development inevitably entailed, and placed a high price on these changes. Modernization was favored, but not at any cost. If it could be achieved with continuity in the society and stability in the economy, that was fine. If it could not, the decision was far from clear. This is not to say that there was any formal or collective decision to resist the pace of modernization set by technical progress and foreign competitors. But the effect of individual reluctance to sacrifice what one had, expressed in economic decisions and in political behavior, was such as to approximate this conservative consensus. We shall shortly examine the question of whether this attitude was unfortunate, but for the time being, let us merely note that the consensus reflected the advanced state of France, her society, her culture, and even her preindustrial economy. There was in fact a great deal to conserve, despite the difficulties of trying to have the best of both old and new.

We can briefly summarize the ways in which the prevailing attitude toward economic development, working through the various elements of our earlier discussion, shaped the economic growth of France. First, and perhaps most important in the long run, technical change was relatively slow, despite a fairly strong contribution to the necessary scientific and technological knowledge on the part of Frenchmen. Because industry and agriculture were, as we have seen, hesitant to engage resources in providing for the future, improvements seldom were fully worked out in France and were slowly adopted after development. A second consequence was that the government did not play a very constructive role, again despite a strong tradition of expert and intelligent civil servants. It was too fully occupied in preserving a delicate and suspicious consensus (or stalemate) between economic forces always on the lookout against attempts to make them pay too large a share of the costs of change to which all were so sensitive.

The financial mechanism, by means of which the vital process of capital formation can achieve its full strength, also felt the effects of "Malthusianism," as the French call exaggerated sensitivity to change and risk. There were important innovations in France, such as the industrial bank, whose role we shall appreciate in studying the German case. But savers were as reluctant to engage their funds in industrial ventures as firms were to submit to the exigencies of control by outside borrowers. So promising ideas went begging for funds, while the thrifty French eagerly bought the bonds of eastern European governments or the low-yielding *rentes* of their own state. Finally, while there were many efficient producers, and most of the new techniques found at least some application, nowhere did France really take advantage of the economic benefits of large-scale production and intense specialization. The Frenchman was truly a Jacques-of-all-trades. The heady whirl of growth made possible in England by the joint development of iron, coal, steam, and cotton found only a pale echo in France, because resources were not massively shifted to the new. The old retained its rights, and every means was used to defer the day when it would be squeezed out.

Why should we be critical of slow growth in France? Are we merely being fashionable, or foolishly consistent in our basic approach of taking economic growth as the guiding thread for our historical survey? There is no question that rapid growth imposes individual hardship and collective loss. England in the Industrial Revolution showed this well, and Soviet Russia was to provide more proof, if needed, in the twentieth century. Perhaps the French were merely proving their cultural superiority in refusing the extreme choices of discarding the past or rejecting the future. There is, I think, something in this. In the opinions of many, French life retained a civilized charm more dynamic countries could not offer, while avoiding the extremes of cruel poverty and backwardness of many Mediterranean countries.

In the long run, however, the equilibrium could not last. The reckoning came in the 1930s. Yet even before World War I, France showed a tendency toward excessive concern with the way the economic pie was divided. This was a natural consequence of slow growth and of the care with which individuals tried to protect their interests from the cold winds of change. The political system, in particular, was largely based on groups formed to protect the economic position of their members, whether farmers, workers, shopkeepers, or manufacturers. It sacrificed the possibility of organizing the community as a whole for large common tasks in favor of granting many groups a veto over any action they felt might threaten them. When economic conditions became really difficult, during the world-wide depression of the 1930s, the opposing groups coalesced into two hostile factions, and civil war became a real possibility. Although it was averted, the consensus on which French society was based had been damaged beyond repair.

France had been threatened before, however. For there was one aspect of French goals that was fundamentally inconsistent with the general desire to keep a tight rein on the upsetting process of development. This was the desire to play a major role in a world dominated by the rivalries of great powers. Such an ambition was too expensive for a country trying to keep its families small, its industries modest, and begrudging the government every franc that did not directly result in tangible advantages to some group. World War I, in which France lost more than a million men as well as most of her impressive portfolio of foreign assets, should have made this clear. Yet the very difficulty of the war, and the great price of the victory, made it politically impossible for the country to drop out of the running. In 1940, France's inadequacies as a great power were dramatically shown by her rapid collapse before the terrible efficiency of the German war machine. Interestingly enough, it was not so much a quantitative lack of men or arms that hurt France, but rather the absence of social cohesion and of commitment to the latest in technology.

The France that emerged from World War II appeared very much unchanged. There was still the political instability, still the predominance of small units of production, still the concern for making sure one's group was not saddled with too much of the general burden. Yet something fundamental *had* changed: the will to grow was there, though it was consciously implemented at first only by a small minority in government and industry. But that story later.

Going back to 1914, what had been accomplished by three quarters of a century of slow modernization? France had her modern sectors, both in agriculture and in industry. The North and the plains around Paris were highly productive, while an expensive and intricate distribution system gathered the tasty products of numerous small farms and fishing ports throughout the country. There were large factories and real industrial regions. The North and the East were the most important, but there were pockets of activity dotted around the Massif Central, in Normandy, and elsewhere. Traditional craftlike industries, emphasizing quality over quantity, continued to provide employment and some exports.

French civil engineers continued a tradition dating back to Louis XIV. Their bridges, dams, railroads, canals, and tunnels—not forgetting the Eiffel Tower—were prominent landmarks of the industrial landscape both in and out of France. Finally, no country was more enthusiastic in its contribution to the early development of airplanes and automobiles, at least until war allowed the United States to take a huge lead after 1914.

We conclude as we began. One can focus on the changes or on the numerous remaining preindustrial aspects of the economy, and judge accordingly. Yet the events of 1914 to 1945 almost compel the critical verdict that the economic development of France in the nineteenth century was not thorough enough, and her growth too slow, for a nation so immersed in power politics. If forced to choose the one change that could have spelled the difference, that could have allowed France to grow sufficiently fast without giving up her commitment to gradualness and balance, I would look for it in technology. The example to cite is that of Switzerland, which compensated for smallness and the virtually complete absence of natural resources by steadfastly pursuing technical excellence. The result was steady economic growth with a minimum of strain on the social fabric and of dislocation in the economic structure. True, Switzerland enjoyed peace and neutrality, but France did not pay any really heavy economic or human price for war until 1914. Until then, at least, she could have retained her family farms and firms, her gradual and limited geographical mobility, and the variety of her landscapes and productions, but only at the cost of devoting sufficient resources to improving efficiency and then adopting the improvements rapidly and fully.

CHAPTER 12

The

Surging Development

of Germany

Germany was a cultural and geographic concept, not a nation, until at least the middle of the nineteenth century. By all the measures of economic strength, the many sovereign states in which German was spoken were then clearly behind France, not to mention England. Yet by 1914 the German Empire had become a powerful and unified industrial giant. Economic development in Germany was, without question, a brilliant success in its own terms. Furthermore, the social consequences of industrialization were perhaps better controlled here than elsewhere, as welfare programs and relative social peace can attest. Nevertheless, in place of the consensus of Britain and the sociopolitical stalemate of France, there was a political near-vacuum in which the state had almost a free hand. Rapid economic growth, by making available a large surplus of resources, allowed a considerable military and colonial buildup, while the rise of a large middle class did not serve to subject the ambitions of the state to any real control. Economic development had not created a pluralistic society in Germany, or if it had, the political expression of pluralism was strongly muted. Our primary concern is with the story of economic growth as such, but it is useful to recall the aggressive policies made possible by this growth, as a reminder that our implicit judgment of the desirability of growth may be subject to caution.

From the economic point of view, Germany presents some revealing contrasts with both Britain and France. In addition to a later start, Germany also had less preparation for modernization than England, where we have noted a long apprenticeship in agriculture, commerce, and social change before 1750. Perhaps for this reason, German development was more organized, less diffuse in its initiatives, than English. The role of great banks and of the state will occupy us particularly in this regard.

There was a curious dualism about the industrial rise of Germany, again by comparison with Britain. On the one hand, the Germans made a lasting commitment to the pursuit of technological sophistication, a commitment that proved particularly fortunate in the last quarter of the nineteenth century. This involved especially the development of those industries whose techniques were based on science. It required considerable investment in education and in research and development, as well as a willingness to make frequent, and often drastic, changes in the methods of production and the composition of output. As we have seen, we could explain to a considerable extent the slowdown in British growth by failures in just this regard. On the other hand, German industry showed a full awareness of its commercial lag, as compared to Britain. The response was a blend of modesty and aggressiveness British sellers found troublesome, as well as a bit distasteful. No market was too small, no language too difficult, no request too outlandish for the German exporter.

In comparison with France, the main contrast is the rapid pace of development, especially in regard to the poorer initial conditions prevailing in Germany. While it is true that crises were sharper east of the Rhine, those of 1857 and 1873 in particular, they were often of shorter duration, and there was exceptionally fast growth in "unspectacular" periods such as the 1860s and 1880s. Short crises and rapid growth even in the absence of particular stimulus from a world boom were the result of the concentrated push in response to new technical opportunities, a push conspicuously absent in the case of France (except perhaps in connection with railroads in the 1850s). Germany enjoyed a succession of such bursts, led by railroads, the opening of the Ruhr, and the beginnings of steel, of industrial organic chemistry, and of electricity. In these booms, the strong dedication to exports was of fundamental importance, since the domestic market was inadequate to absorb the full increase in output with sufficient speed and smoothness.

But let us turn back to the period before development, and trace briefly the course of economic change in Germany. This will also give us a clue to the nationalistic bias in the use Germany made of her economic gains. For unity was the great preoccupation even before there was any hint of modern economic growth. Germany had lost the very loose cohesion formerly provided by the Holy Roman Emperor in the struggles that followed the Reformation and persisted for a century. The worst of these, the Thirty Years' War (1618–1648), had cost her more, however, than political fragmentation. Something like one half the total population had been killed, and the economy correspondingly devastated. Germany had been the battlefield of competing political and religious factions and powers in wars far more deadly to the civilian population than to fighting men. Disease, murder, and starvation had claimed many more lives than the awkward firearms of the time.

The small and weak German states emerging from this holocaust were all ruled absolutely, by a king, a duke, or even a bishop. When they were not imitating the splendors of the French court, these princes took an active hand in the reconstruction of their domains, especially in the revival of agriculture. They also promoted repopulation, and in particular welcomed refugees, such as the French Huguenots after their expulsion (1685) from France. The economic activity of the state was modeled on the mercantilist policies of the West, though foreign trade played a smaller part.[5] Although the princes strove to promote some industrial ventures, their main achievement was to replace the regulation of the economy by guilds and local authorities with strict tutelage that was at least uniform over their territory.

But Germany remained broken up and trade continued to be an obstacle course, with frequent tolls and customs as well as conflicting policies and monetary systems. It took the Napoleonic conquest to give the first major push toward unity. Napoleon's Confederation of the Rhine, though later rejected as an external imposition, did effect a large permanent reduction in the number of German states.

Nonetheless, progress toward development was slower after 1815 than in France. Germany was poorer, and her small market was still badly fragmented. Agricultural depression after the return of peace in 1815 also contributed to the delay in this predominantly agricultural country. In fact, it is more nearly accurate to speak of an industrial "revolution" in Germany than in England, for the Germans had none of the prerequisites, such as highly developed foreign commerce, an established export industry, and a substantial middle class of improving landlords and experienced merchants.

The most obviously positive factor during the period before the 1840s was the ambition of Prussia to take the lead in a unified Germany, and the realization that this enterprise would require considerable economic strengthening of the country. The methods of the Prussian government were a continuation of the cameralist tradition, involving considerable state help but also close supervision. Yet we must be

---

[5] The equivalent of mercantilism in small and land-locked states has been called cameralism.

careful, for the actual beginnings of industrialization do not bear out the view that Prussian efficiency, exercised through disciplined civil servants, was the real motor of development.

Without a doubt, the Prussian plan worked very well in the matter of unifying Germany, although the full enterprise took until 1870, and even then did not include Austria. In 1833, Prussia joined with a number of neighboring states to form the *Zollverein,* or customs union. This abolished tariffs between all member states and imposed on them the common external tariff of Prussia, which happened to be relatively low. While there was supposedly complete preservation of the several sovereignties, the impetus of customs union led to gradual fusion of policies and practices in many spheres, such as money, and eventually to full political union. (Whether this must be the case in a customs union is a matter of more than idle interest in today's Europe.) In any case, despite the loss of autonomy involved, most German states eventually joined the *Zollverein* or its successor North German Confederation. Full union became a reality in the nationalistic euphoria of the victory over France: the Empire was proclaimed in Versailles in 1871. There is no question of the beneficial effects, for trade and finance directly and for all economic activity eventually, of the *Zollverein.* But the customs union only rectified an absurd situation in Central Europe, and we would be in error to hold it responsible for the industrial surge of Germany after the mid-century.

For the moment, let us look at certain areas in which the influence of the state was far from decisive, if not actually negative. The first sizable development of industry in Germany took place in the Silesian coal and iron fields and the state had a very direct hand in it. However, Silesian industry, though often of large scale, had an unenviable record of technical performance and economic success. The real beginnings of German industrial development date from the railroad boom of the 1840s and from the development of the

Ruhr coal basin after the abortive revolution of 1848. In both cases, the Prussian government, dismayed by what it considered speculative excesses, acted to *curtail* company formation and capital mobilization through stock markets. While some ventures were imprudent, of course, when the smoke had cleared and the unsound firms had been shaken out, the usual outcome of a speculative burst was a legacy of real capital, of shafts sunk, lines built, or factories put up. There might be sadder but wiser investors and bankrupt entrepreneurs or promoters, but someone took over the real capital, with new financing, and the economy enjoyed the benefits of additional productive capacity. Finally, we should note that government intervention was as great in the southern states as in Prussia, whereas development lagged behind.

Therefore, private initiative was indeed a potent factor behind German industrialization. With regard to the role of the state, we must strive to escape mythology. Because Prussia was so marked by the military discipline of its bureaucracy and by a social order that seemed to bespeak close control of the whole country by the state, we are tempted to view development as having proceeded largely from the government.[6]

The state did help, in the period of industrialization, by its continued concern with the economy. Railroad lines were not allowed to disappear, or even be delayed, because of bankruptcy, nor did the private economy have to suffer from neglect of public services or from excessive devotion to routine in economic regulation.

We are purposefully giving little emphasis to the question of natural resources, but we must mention the favorable impact of the Ruhr as a contributing factor along with enterprise and government action. Unlike many of the French coal fields, it turned out to be a large basin and able to supply good coking coal at moderate cost.

[6] Inversely, our view of German recovery from the ravages of World War II will have to go behind the panegyrics of the Germans in praise of the free market, and take note of the considerable role played by the government in the "economic miracle."

Before pursuing our survey of industrial developments, let us review briefly the changes taking place in agriculture. This sector played a smaller role in German development than it had in England, but its progress was at least sufficient to avoid exerting a negative influence, as it did in France during this period.

We must distinguish two, and perhaps three, agricultures in Germany. The West need not detain us long, for it was markedly similar to France in agrarian structure. In its northern part there were substantial farms, whereas in the south they tended to be of suboptimal size, and technical improvements were correspondingly slow to spread. Everywhere in western Germany peasant ownership or modern tenancy consolidated its hold in the first half of the nineteenth century. The French Revolution had begun the process and it continued after 1815 with more gradual arrangements, involving compensation, for removing the remnants of feudalism.

East of the Elbe things were different. The land was held in large estates, often by members of the military aristocracy. A number of factors favored change early in the nineteenth century. The serfs, for such the peasants still were, had been promised relief in exchange for their support in the war against Napoleon. Grain production from these regions was needed, particularly as exports to pay for imports of industrial goods from England. Finally, there was the special location of the grain lands at the frontier with Slavic countries that were an economic as well as a cultural threat in German eyes.

Thus, the agrarian problem in the East was of central importance. The solution tended to sacrifice social considerations for economic efficiency and political ends. Serfdom was in fact ended, but the cost of freedom was high enough to turn many of the peasants into landless laborers, while the great estates were correspondingly enlarged. This arrangement was challenged by the flight of workers to urban factories or to empty lands outside Germany to the south and east, while the influx of Polish replacement labor was considered dangerous for the continued Germanness ɔf the Eastern regions. One answer was a policy of colonization, whereby farmers were given lands in the East to consolidate the German presence.

Despite the tensions of change in land tenure, German agriculture did make considerable progress, particularly in the periods of relatively high prices (1850–1873 and 1896–1913). There were three important factors in this technical improvement, as usual related to one another. One was the use of chemical fertilizers, especially important in view of the mediocre soils in much of Germany. This is in turn partially traceable to the progress of the chemical industry, and especially to its efforts in developing and diffusing the techniques of fertilizer use. Second, agricultural education and extension were also powerfully supported by the state in the form of schools of all levels, experiment stations, and local services. The last element was the cooperative movement, aimed at breaking the social and economic isolation of the farmer. Cooperatives provided joint buying and selling services, insurance and savings schemes, and credit facilities. Their purpose was especially to free the German peasant from the merchant-money lender, frequently a Jew, who was thought to exploit him. Certainly, the new system had considerable advantages of scale.

In the first period of growth, until the crisis of 1873, Germany continued to export food. Agricultural progress involved mainly the improvement of crop rotations on the English model, and the spread of new productions, particularly the sugar beet and the potato. The crash of 1873, coinciding with the arrival on European markets of cheap grain, first from Eastern Europe and then from overseas, forced a sharp change in German trade policy. She became protectionist, and agriculture fought now to retain the home market. But German protectionism was never so sweeping as French. Industry exported too much to make widespread industrial protection possible, while dear bread, or food, would have been a great burden on industrial profits. So a compromise was reached. The politically powerful Prussian landlords obtained moderate protection, but they were clearly aware of the limits to the advantage they could hope for over foreign producers, and made great efforts to improve productivity. By 1914, Germany was importing some 20 percent of her food, although the last two decades had seen a great spurt of mechanization in agriculture, favored by the improvement in world prices.

The relative position of agriculture had steadily declined, but there had been enough absolute progress so that industrialization was not retarded. Thus, Germany was largely freed from having to choose either the English or the French horn of the dilemma brought about by the crisis of 1873—to abandon agriculture or to let it drag down the whole economy by protection or subsidy.

As we have mentioned, industrial development really began with the development of railroads and with the opening of the Ruhr. Before this, there had been a considerable domestic industry, doomed to lose importance, and a weak textile sector, in addition to the Silesian iron and coal works. The new industrial structure had a number of centers. Some were based on natural resources, such as the Ruhr and, later, the brown coal fields of central Germany. Others were located on rivers or near harbors, especially the chemical and food-processing industries. The large towns, which were growing at a tremendous rate, concentrated labor-using mechanical and electrical plants.

There was even a considerable revival of the old craft industries, once they made the necessary adjustments. Increased incomes provided a market for luxury goods, while the development of small electric motors gave small workshops a new lease on life. Finally, even mighty industrial plants needed the services of repairmen, tool- and diemakers, and craftsmen to make instruments and prototypes.

Although Germany did not neglect the established industries, such as textiles and iron, she showed particular strength in newer branches. The German entrepreneur believed in science, though not often a scientist himself, and he was willing to back his belief with money and patience. Thus, a chemical firm spent more than $6 million (of the time) and eighteen years working out the process for making synthetic indigo, nature's last holdout among the important dyestuffs. But we can cite similar exploits in a long list of industries, from steel to drugs and from electrical machinery to internal-combustion engines and artificial textiles.

The Germans were particularly on the lookout for ways of decreasing their dependence on foreign sources of supply for essential raw materials, since they foresaw an armed conflict with the Mistress of the Seas across the North Sea. For example, they were eager to find a way of making nitrogen fertilizers, until then imported from Chile. By coincidence, the process was worked out in 1913. It was a coincidence, since ammonia and the nitrates derived from it were indispensable to the making of munitions. Without any question, the Germans would have been unable to sustain an intensive (and unforeseen) four-year war in the absence of their newly found source of nitrates.

A striking feature of German industry was bigness, due partly to the expenses of research and the need for large units of capital. It was also a matter of style, however. Not only were individual plants and firms large, but they also tended to group into cartels, arrangements for sharing the market and maintaining stable prices. Despite the government's approval, the cartels were not highly durable, for the stable price was very much worth undercutting and the Germans were not averse to profits. Thus, cartels tended to be transformed into more formal and binding arrangements, resembling American trusts. The movement was accelerated by the difficult times of the 1920s, when great *Konzerne* were formed, such as the IG-Farben trust in chemicals.

However, reduced competition inside Germany did not seriously blunt the drive for greater efficiency and technical progress. For one thing, the Germans believed in efficiency:

they used the latest techniques as a matter of principle rather than calculation. But the main force was the constant concern for exporting. For foreign trade is more than an opportunity to specialize, valuable as the resulting economies of scale are. It is also the best way to keep an industry "honest" and to avoid recourse to uneconomic arrangements for allowing producers to live the quiet life.

How could a poor country, for Germany was poor in 1850, finance so rapid an industrialization? We must remember that capital requirements had vastly increased since the days of England's industrial beginnings. The banking system was the answer, in particular the industrial banks.

To understand the role of the industrial banks, consider briefly the function of a bank. Originally, banks were repositories for valuables. When the keeper of these safe places saw that he always had a considerable sum on hand, he began to lend out part of it, retaining only enough to meet the demand of his depositors. Of course, two conditions are necessary for this process to be viable: first, only some of the depositors can exercise their claims at any one time, as the banker can never satisfy all at once; second, over a long period, new deposits must at least balance out the pace of withdrawals. The basic difference between loans and deposits is that the banker has to pay off his depositors at once, on demand, while he collects his loans only as they come due. It is this feature of a bank which is crucial for our purposes: its liabilities (deposits) are liquid, that is, payable at short notice, while its assets (loans) are less liquid. As we know, the thing is workable, because deposits are not claimed often and loans are spaced out.[7]

In France and England, the principal banks considered it prudent to keep their loans fairly liquid, although of course less so than their deposits. This meant making safe loans for a short time. Private banks used their owners' and depositors' funds to lend for longer periods, but they chose their customers with care and personal knowledge.

[7] Peter L. Bernstein, *A Primer on Money, Banking, and Gold* (New York: Random House, 1965).

In all this, there was no room for the financing of new industrial ventures, where the entrepreneur had no security but an idea and lots of energy, and where he would realize no profits for a long time even if he were successful. We have seen that the English pioneers of the Industrial Revolution managed to find the small sums they needed by individual contact with prosperous backers, but this was an inadequate mechanism for the long run. A later solution was the joint-stock company, or corporation, in which many owners pooled comparatively small amounts of capital and agreed to share in the profits rather than claim their money back. But while this worked well for utilities, such as railroads and gasworks, or for established companies, it did not help newcomers to any extent.

The origins of industrial banks, banks that would help launch industrial ventures, go back to Belgium in the 1830s, but it was the Crédit Mobilier in France (1852) that made the institution known and the Germans who made it work. The key to their success was size. Because the German industrial banks were large, they could have enough irons in the fire to cut down their risks considerably. They also spread their risks by undertaking all kinds of banking business, in addition to providing "venture capital." Finally, they protected themselves by becoming expert in industrial and commercial problems and by supervising the companies to whom they had made long-term loans. For we must remember that the minor role of banks in French industrialization, and perhaps in English, was due in large part to the dislike felt by entrepreneurs for bank supervision. Whether the Germans were less interested in their independence, or whether it was a luxury the relatively poor country could not afford, remains an open question.

In any case, German industry was strongly backed and guided by the big industrial banks, who encouraged the close organization of industry through cartels, trusts, chambers of commerce, trade associations, and other organizations. Nor has this feature disappeared from the German economy in recent times. It is still normal for the board of directors of large firms to include at least one banker, while banks act as stockbrokers and collect proxy votes before annual stockholders' meetings. In this way, German banks have tempered the force of competition, whether for good or bad, and the state has not been the sole agent interfering with the free play of unrestricted markets.

Quite obviously, German industry could not have developed as it did without a parallel push in transportation. Furthermore, physical unification of the Fatherland tied in well with the political and cultural drive for unity. So it is not surprising to see Germany rapidly building railroads and also undertaking great projects for the improvement of internal navigation. In railroads, the urge to build overshadowed the concern for thoroughness and quality. The lines were almost American in the rapid and slapdash way they were built, quite different from the solid British roads. But it did not matter. Technical progress was so rapid that everything had to be replaced several times in any case. By the 1880s, when railroads were a stable institution, Germany had an efficient network managed by a near-military corps of employees. Actual ownership remained with the individual states, sometimes even in private hands, but operations were centralized, and very Prussian.

In a sense, Germany's transportation benefited at first from her lack of unity. Instead of long and drawn-out plans, as in France, somewhat disorganized and competitive activity burst forth in the various states of the future Empire, both in rail and in water transport. Later on the pieces were joined together in a more organized fashion, and the result was a more balanced system as well as more rapid development.

Ironically, the great ports of the North, the proud Hanse towns, were among the last to join the economic unit called Germany. Perhaps this too helped, by limiting the inflow of British goods while German industry was still in its apprentice stage. Later, these same harbors were the gateways of Germany's drive for export markets. The combination of their commercial and seafaring tradition and of the German lead in steel and propulsion technology made the Reich a serious contender for supremacy in merchant shipping, and a clear second to England in any case.

Perhaps the most remarkable fact about German development is the limited degree to which economic change interacted with other aspects of the society. We have seen that England converted her social and political structure so as to conform to the needs of a mobile and growing economy, even though the trappings of the old order, the aristocracy in particular, were retained. In France, on the other hand, we have had evidence of economic change being retarded by social conservatism and also by the delicate political balance between those who did and those who did not accept the changes wrought by the Revolution of 1789.

In Germany, the old order retained much of its force, and yet this seemed not to exert any restrictive influence on economic growth. Nor did industrialization appear to affect the country's social and political organization. The only attempt at radical political change, a minor one at that, was made in 1848, before any real start in development had been made. And the socialist movement, though as large as any in Europe, was preoccupied with doctrinal conflicts and remained of secondary significance in terms of political power. At the popular level, Germany still stressed the old values of a peasant society, even though by 1910 60 percent of the population was urban. The parallel with Japan is striking. In both countries industrialization proceeded with great rapidity, despite serious initial backwardness, and the social order was modified surprisingly little. Furthermore, we do not need to be told that both countries placed their industrial strength at the service of an aggressive foreign policy.

CHAPTER 13 ~~~~~~

The "Underdeveloped" Countries of Southern and Eastern Europe

T hus far, we have considered the industrialization of the three major powers of Western Europe, dominating the European economic scene in the late nineteenth century through the combined effects of size and productive power. What of the others? We can divide them into two groups, although thereby doing less than justice to the richness and diversity of their experience. Both groups consist of countries that played a secondary part in economic life, in the trade and rivalries of the age, but for different reasons. Some countries were fairly advanced, but too small to rival the major powers. The others were sometimes large, but in all cases backward. The first group lay in northern Europe, the second in the southern and eastern part of the Continent. Two countries in the second group departed from these generalizations: Ireland, because of its location, and Russia, which almost attained the rank of a major economic power.

Economic historians have unfairly neglected the small advanced countries of Europe, and we shall do little to rectify this. Yet within the limits imposed by size, and perhaps by sense, they modernized steadily, and growth in per capita incomes kept pace with that in the industrial giants, or even exceeded it. The common characteristic of the Scandinavian countries, Holland, and Switzerland was the pursuit of comparative advantage based on resources and skills, particularly the latter. For they had to trade if they wished to enjoy the benefits of mass-produced textiles, of iron and steel and their many products, and of cheap grain. Size precluded the development at home of the complete spectrum of industries. Their industrial trade emphasized products that complemented, rather than competed directly with, those of the larger countries, so that growth elsewhere generated opportunities for them more often than it posed a threat. The quality steels of Sweden, the instruments and dyestuffs of Switzerland, and the merchant marines of Norway and the Netherlands are cases in point.

Continuing attention to expanding and improving traditional production was equally important for the small advanced countries, especially production deriving from the so-called "primary" sector of agriculture, fishing, and forestry. Even more than the large countries, the small ones relied on ever fuller use and greater transformation of their resources. For while the general importance of natural resources diminishes as economies grow and industrialize, it is also true that demand shifts toward more highly processed raw materials. Indeed, all manufacturing is in fact no more than the processing of natural products. The northern countries paid particular attention to the technology of primary production and to new ways of processing primary products. The results are still too familiar to need enumeration— from the tulips and cheeses of Holland to the bacon and butter of Denmark and the herring and wood pulp of the Scandinavian Peninsula. In some cases, specialized processing gave these countries a comparative advantage in products for which they had no resources, the chocolate of Holland and Switzerland being a good example. Markets were provided by the rapid increases in incomes in neighboring lands, translated into substantial breakfasts, morning newspapers, suburban gardens, and widespread nibbling of sweets. Careful attention to quality, skill, and education permitted these countries to remain competitive despite their small size, and to reconcile efficiency and economic change with remarkable social and cultural stability.

Perhaps their most striking feature, from the point of view of the traveler, has been the harmony and continuity of their development, the blending of old and new in buildings and landscapes. This is in major part due to resolute avoidance of wars, but let us also recognize that economic change can scar the land as harshly as battles. Nowhere has economic development been so well harnessed as in these small countries of Europe. It is a lesson to be pondered today by those who fear that growth must mean the total destruction of non-Western cultures. Perhaps the old and the new can be reconciled outside Europe too, but only at real cost in terms of education, of political restraint, and of community spirit. The small countries of northern and western Europe show that industrial landscapes need not be ugly, that rural life need not be "idiotic," in the words of Marx, and that large neighbors need not dominate a small nation.

The French say that "happy peoples have no history," and it is true that we do not have much to offer by way of explanation for the successes we have just noted. The relative, and often absolute, economic failures of the second group of countries, the laggards, have been more closely studied. The lessons of unsuccessful, delayed, or difficult development are particularly relevant today, when the problems of backward nations outside Europe, the developing countries as they are optimistically (and sometimes euphemistically) called, are the prime concern of economics.

More than analogy ties the two groups, however. In the nineteenth century, eastern and southern Europe was the underdeveloped fringe of the industrial world: backward,

troubled in its political and social life, the battleground for
rival great powers who preferred to avoid direct confrontations. Just as the cold war has been fought more in the
Congo and Vietnam than in Europe, so Italy and then the
Balkans were the powder kegs of Europe in the increasingly
tense "peaceful" nineteenth century (as Spain turned out to
be in a later time).

There are other parallels, too. One of the seminal contributions to the now-fashionable discipline of economic development was written during World War II with specific
reference to Southern and Eastern Europe.[8] Finally, it is
here that socialism was first tried as an alternative road to
development in place of the largely capitalist system of
Western Europe. Today, many developing countries are
nominally socialistic, even though they are in fact trying to
work with more or less uneasy amalgams of the two systems,
while the systems themselves are rapidly losing their ideological purity in the advanced countries as well.

At first sight, the backward countries of Southern and
Eastern Europe (essentially the southern peninsulas of the
Continent, plus everything east of Germany) appeared to
remain "traditional" societies in the nineteenth century,
with beginnings of modern economic activity here and
there. This conception results from too simple a view of
development as the only important economic episode. It neglects the varieties and complexities of preindustrial economies. Hopefully, the reader of this book, in which the story
of European economic growth has been carried back to the
beginning of the Christian Era, will find it easy to reject the
view that economic history can consist merely in analyzing
the development process and describing the economy "before" and "after." We must attempt a somewhat more sophisticated level of oversimplification and generalization!

At the start of the nineteenth century, most of the region
lived under an essentially feudal system, with a serflike
peasantry, a landowning aristocracy, and little urban or
middle-class development. There were exceptions, in partic-

8 By Professor P. N. Rosenstein-Rodan.

ular the regions touching on the growth leaders to the west, such as northern Italy, Catalonia, and German-speaking Austria. Elsewhere, the economy was held back by the archaic agrarian system, in which few incentives and fewer possibilities for progress existed, and by the rigid social stratification which accompanied it.

During the century, considerable change in the agrarian system, and thus in economic life, took place, but the primary consequence was most often rapid population growth that persistently tended to outrun the expansion in output. In some cases, however, there was considerable partial development. We shall examine the changes, grouping regions for simplicity, and consider the role played by contact with more advanced economies and by governments, especially in the case of Russian development.

The old system of agriculture rested on an oppressed peasantry, while the landowning class usually relied on the size of its estates and the harshness of its agents for sufficient income. Thus, the nobility had no great need to seek improved productivity, and the peasantry, besides lacking in education and capital, had learned that any improvement merely attracted the attention of bailiffs and tax collectors. Fortunately, agricultural land was often relatively abundant until the late nineteenth century, so that living standards, though low, were not everywhere near starvation levels. For later developments, we can distinguish the areas of foreign oppression, such as those under Turkish rule, from regions more like eastern Germany in which the aristocracy was native. Spain, southern Italy, Hungary, and Czarist Russia were of the latter type.

The distinction is important in view of the way the agrarian system changed in the nineteenth century. Where the land had been owned by foreigners, independence was accompanied by land reform, and owner-worked peasant farms became the rule. Serbia and Bulgaria were typical cases. But the model also fits liberation from the tyranny of a native aristocracy by means of a revolution, meaning a true social upheaval such as occurred in France in 1789 and

in Russia in 1917. For this reason we may call this the
"French" model. As in France, peasant agriculture was not
conducive to growth, because there was little specialization,
not much demand for industrial goods, and slow progress of
technology. But society was relatively stable, and the standard of living far from uniformly miserable, despite the
highly rustic mode of life. Besides fitting Serbia and Bulgaria, this is not a bad description of Soviet agriculture in
the period of the New Economic Policy, that is, from the
end of civil war until collectivization by Stalin in 1928. The
main difference between Eastern Europe and France, besides, of course, the much greater development of towns and
industry in the latter, was the former's absence of demographic restraint. As the nineteenth century progressed, increases in output were absorbed by a growing population,
and fields tended to become badly split up at the same time
as unemployment or underemployment increased.

When the landowning aristocracy was native and remained in power, the impetus to change came through the
opening of markets, usually to the west, for agricultural
products. Hungary is the classic case of an aristocracy made
aware of the opportunities for gain from exporting to the
industrial regions. As in eastern Germany, the serfs were
liberated, but under conditions ensuring the survival, or
even progression, of large estates farmed with abundant
peasant labor. On the basis of export earnings and of contact
with more advanced regions, an urban industrial sector
arose, although the rural masses had no contact with it.

If we replace the Hungarian nobility by the Russian
state, and the growth of Budapest, with its varied industries
and its charm and culture, by the start of a heavy-industry
complex and the building of a railroad network, we have
here a good sketch of the development of Czarist Russia
after 1860, to which we shall return. In both cases a dual
economy grew up, based on the exchange of agricultural exports for foreign capital, techniques, and equipment. The
foreign contributions and the increased incomes of the
upper classes supported a modern urban-industrial com-

plex, while rural areas were exploited more severely. This development was much more limited in Hungary and Russia than in Germany, since technical progress was insufficient in agriculture, and probably also in industry, to draw the rest of the economy gradually into the modern sector.

For completeness, we must also mention the areas that failed to make any substantial progress, in particular southern Italy and most of Spain. Despite considerable, though still spotty, industrial development in a few regions, these countries retained the *latifundia,* that is, the great estates supporting the nobles (and the Church) in style, despite poor techniques, and the *minifundia,* or perilously small peasant holdings. Development in the "North:" Lombardy and Piedmont, Asturias and Catalonia, relied very little on the surplus from the backward regions. Foreign goods, for investment or to allow the urban classes a truly European mode of life, were exchanged for minerals and agricultural crops grown in a commercial farming sector such as the Levant in Spain and the Po plain in Italy. There was also considerable borrowing from advanced countries.

Neither Spain nor Italy suffered from any one major obstacle to development. Rather, they were somewhat deficient in a number of respects: resources, scale of markets, social cohesion, education, and the value attached to industry and profit in the culture. Spain failed to profit from many decades of external, if not internal, peace, while political unification had only a limited economic impact in Italy. We are largely forced to rely on unpleasantly nonverifiable explanations of backwardness, such as absence of the capitalist spirit, an inappropriate value system, or the supposed inherent inferiority of Catholicism for economic growth, in contrast to the Protestant Ethic.

In all the backward parts of Europe, such industrial development as did take place relied on close associations with neighboring advanced countries. Capital was raised in London and Paris. The firms were often owned by foreigners, or at least Westernized locals, when they were not simply subsidiaries of German, Swiss, or English companies. Managers and technicians were also imported, or at least trained abroad, and the techniques they implemented reflected the conditions they had experienced there rather than the local environment.

The question is whether such "imported" industrial and commercial development had as great an impact on the overall modernization of the economy as a more spontaneous and indigenous drive might have had. We do not know, but the problem is raised too frequently in the nationalistic context of today's development push (outside Europe) to be ignored completely. It is probably fair to say that the immediate choice was not between foreign-inspired development and something more home-grown, but rather between what occurred and nothing. But some would argue that foreigners, by using their easy access to the resources of industrial countries, skimmed the most readily available profit opportunities and made the job harder for local enterprise. This is the thesis of "informal imperialism," which also alleges that foreign enterprise resists the political and social transformations that are a prerequisite for true development. However valid the thesis may be, we must note that the economic importance of such backward countries to the great trading nations in the late nineteenth century was immeasurably greater than that of the new overseas colonies they rushed to acquire in the last great wave of colonial expansion, or "formal" imperialism.

One country stands out from the group and deserves our special attention. This is the Czarist Empire of Russia. In many ways it was highly backward, and the per capita income of its people was undoubtedly lower than that of any but the most stagnant regions of Europe, such as the southern parts of Spain and Italy and perhaps the mountainous portions of the Balkans. Yet it was a large and comparatively unified and stable political entity, a partner in the Treaty of Vienna of 1815 that had set the map of Europe, and a principal in the involved diplomatic and military confrontations attendant on the decline of the Ottoman and Austrian empires. In addition, Russia underwent a particularly spectacular burst of partial industrial development in the late nineteenth century, made possible by its size, its mineral resources, and the international ambitions of its rulers. We have already indicated the basic mechanism of this development: stepped-up appropriation of the agricultural surplus in a reorganized agrarian regime, exports to the West in exchange for contributions to industrialization, and the growth of a dual economy.

The special nature of the Russian case stems from the government's role in the process. To begin with, although the liberation of the serfs in 1861 was supposed to profit the nobles, as happened in Hungary and Prussia, the Russian landowners were usually so far in debt that the state, in fact, collected the price paid by the peasants for their freedom. In addition, the state made up for the lack of a sufficient market for industrial goods. Because there was no large urban middle class and the rural areas were too backward to absorb much by way of manufactures, the government simply bought the goods itself, and indeed organized and ran the factories in many cases. Textile plants produced uniforms and blankets for the army, while the iron and steel works made weapons and railroad equipment.

This was, of course, not the sum total of Russian industry up until World War I, but whatever private development was encouraged remained secondary. So long as the agricultural sector could be taxed, and the grain so collected exported, foreign machinery and technicians would continue to develop Russian heavy industry, and foreign investors would retain confidence in the safety of their loans. In France, in particular, Russian government bonds formed an important part of the portfolio of assets, and there were few towns, no matter how remote, where the substantial citizens did not own them. The French banks, so reluctant to tie up their funds in dubious (they thought) newfangled industries, had no hesitation in pushing such foreign investments, because they acted only as middlemen and got their

generous commission whatever the long-term fate of the securities.

What this fate was it is hardly necessary to recall. In the
first decade of the twentieth century, however, it looked as if
Russia would extend her development in a healthy way.
More and more private firms were growing up in the ever
larger towns and cities, and some real gains in agricultural
productivity were finally being realized, thanks to important reforms associated with the minister Stolypin. Because
heavy industry was so closely tied to the government, plants
had been built on a large scale from the start, and Russian
practice was by no means inferior. Nonetheless, there were
severe social pressures in Russia, essentially due to continued low levels of consumption for peasants and industrial
workers. These pressures were heightened by economic
crises, particularly in the first decade of the twentieth century, and were brought to the boiling point by unsuccessful
wars in 1905 and 1914–1917.

After three revolutions, a new state emerged, the first in
history to apply socialist ideas to the actual running of an
economy. The state was to own the "means of production,"
meaning all substantial productive units such as factories,
utilities, and commercial financial organizations. Private
property and enterprise would retain only a residual role—
in small workshops and, for a time, in agriculture. For some
ten years after the revolution of 1917, civil war and the need
to consolidate made the Russian economy mark time. In
1928, under the direct leadership of Stalin, the harsh and
powerful socialist pattern for centralized development was
unfolded, and the Soviet Union resumed its rapid industrialization. This story will be told in Part III, but, despite a new social setting, it retains many of the economic
features of Russian development before 1917.

CHAPTER 14 ∽∽∽∽∽

The International
Economy of the Late
Nineteenth Century

Although our discussion of development has followed the progress of individual countries, one of the striking changes ushered in by industrialization was increased interdependence among the nations of Europe and between that continent and others.

The international economy of trade in the Middle Ages and the mercantile era had affected the bulk of economic activity only marginally. Goods from afar merely supplemented consumption based on local production, and few people relied mainly on distant markets to absorb their own specialized output. In the late nineteenth century, however, the progress of trade, industry, agriculture, banking, and especially transport locked economic units into complex structures of interaction. We shall consider here the character of the new international economy and also discern two changes that augured the twentieth century: a new burst of technological advance and the growing economic function of governments.

The most obvious feature of the international economy was the predominance of Europe, and more especially of Britain. The "old" continent had come a long way from the days when it was a secondary market and a source of raw materials and slaves for the more advanced Near and Middle East. Now Europeans made economic decisions at both ends of the long trade lines.[9] The non-Europeans, excepting some British Dominions and the United States, contributed land and labor at low prices; while these low prices limited the possibilities of selling European manufactures, they also kept down the price of raw materials for Europe.

Because Europe, and Britain in particular, were so dominant, their economic system naturally was also predominant. So the international economy was capitalistic. The reader may wonder at finding himself, having reached the late nineteenth century in a book on economic history, with hardly any mention of this great "ism." There is no more slippery or "loaded" concept for the economic historian, and I have felt that insistence on defining capitalism and tracing its development would detract from the story rather than add to it. Now that it is time to sum up the period of European development, we can allow the term on stage for a quick bow.

What is capitalism? On the one hand, it refers to a system of decentralized enterprise in a competitive market economy based on private ownership of the means of production. We have repeatedly stressed the energizing role of entrepreneurial initiative based on material self-interest as well as the allocative efficiency of free markets. Traces of such a system in the European economies appeared far back in the Middle Ages, while political and social constraints on economic enterprise never disappeared. Therefore, we can find no precise separation between a precapitalist and a capitalist period. On the other hand, capitalism refers to the massive use of *capital*, embodied in the tools and processes, the structures and scale of modern industry, agriculture, and trade, regardless of the ownership structure. As such,

[9] See page 133 for a description of the role of London in world trade.

capitalism is the "after" of development, whatever the legal and social framework.

By the late nineteeth century, the second aspect was beginning to overshadow the first, and—especially according to Marxist doctrine—even to conflict with it. As we shall see, the very power and size of economic enterprise made the independent entrepreneur, who did not control his markets and whom society did not control, less and less relevant. Still, most business was carried on through the market by firms in private hands. This capitalism, however, was not entirely industrial. More and more of the working population left agriculture, but the number in manufacturing did not take up all the slack. The development of markets and the scale and capital associated with modern production had given rise to a host of new ventures that did not produce goods at all. A mysterious—to some, sinister—network of "service" firms existed seemingly by shuffling papers and exchanging them. The importance of such intermediaries— bankers, stockbrokers, courtiers, agents, wholesalers, speculators, journalists—was a tribute to the productive powers of modern technology and to the role of organization in coordinating and improving these powers.

Information was thus a necessary condition for the functioning of the international economy, but it would have been useless without *mobility;* for the essence of the system was the willingness of resources to respond to information, always in search of economic advantage.

First of all, goods were mobile. Trade, both within a country's borders and between countries, expanded far more rapidly than output. An estimate of international trade, for which reasonable statistics are available, suggests an increase from $2 billion to $3 billion between 1815 and 1840, and then a dramatic rise to $40 billion by 1914. The basic pattern of mercantile trade was retained, and indeed strengthened. The European countries sold manufactures and imported raw materials. But now the flow relied on comparative costs rather than on the colonial system: because the "backward" countries could not make industrial goods so cheaply, they sold raw materials and food. European capital, technology, and management were available largely to develop mines and plantations that retained and developed the pattern of specialization. There was less need for formal monopolies, navigation laws, and the like.

How free was trade? Compared to the mercantile system, it was very free indeed. For one thing, even where certain colonial markets were reserved for the home country—and this was secondary except for France—any citizen of the country could trade in these markets; the monopoly positions of the great "companies" were gone, although some continued to dominate certain far-flung and hard-to-reach markets. Trade was also free, for the simple reason that the greatest trading nation levied no tariffs. Yet even when a country adopted a protectionist policy, trade remained much freer than it had been in previous centuries or would be after World War I. The levying of tariffs, although it reduced the inflow of particular goods, was a relatively mild restraint compared to the panoply of quotas, prohibitions, exchange controls, and plain administrative roadblocks that would hamper and stifle international trade in the 1930s. Before 1914, most nations applied the "most favored nation" principle, extending to all countries trading concessions negotiated with one partner. This, too, limited the extent of protection.

Thus, the second half of the nineteenth century, with its Edwardian Indian summer, appears as the heyday of unrestricted multilateral trade based on freely convertible currencies. Within the period, however, there was a time of increasing freedom, up to 1870 or so, and an ebb from then on.

By 1914, protection had again become generalized except for England, and there, too, many voices joined Joseph Chamberlain in calling for a retreat from free trade. France and the United States had been lukewarm and temporary converts to free trade, and quickly retreated to protection. But the one was a minor industrial trader, and the other relied primarily on its huge and fast-expanding home market. The German government also seemed to delight in the bureaucratic opportunities afforded by a complex system of tariffs, but the industrial strength of Germany, and her need to export, limited the actual economic significance of the Reich's commercial policy.

Tariffs were the first instruments of a more active economic policy, as well as the weapons of a rear guard action against social and economic change. Advocates of protection used a variety of arguments from the preservation of the family farm to national security, and from sophisticated growth arguments to simplistic calls for making foreigners pay. In the end, however, a particular tariff was adopted chiefly because the domestic producers cared more than the customers, for whom this was only one item of expenditure. The general interest for low prices was diffuse, while the particular concern for *one* higher price was sharply focused. Only where free trade was a dogma, a matter of principle, was the pressure resisted. The major industrial powers nevertheless expanded their trade, and tariffs did not seriously blunt the force of comparative advantage.

The newer industrial countries were another matter. To some extent, they used tariffs as a way of financing government expenditures, since other taxes were hard to levy. But they also tried to encourage industrialization, and this meant keeping the formidable European competitors at bay. Most of the fledgling industries, in the Balkans, Italy, South America, and so on, produced consumer goods, especially textiles. For this reason, Britain felt the new competitive pressure most. Over-all, the beginnings of development outside the industrial "heartland" did not diminish the flow of trade, for the new industries required machinery, chemicals, and trained personnel. But the changing composition of trade emphasized the need for the industrial powers to keep their economic structure flexible and up to date.

It should not be thought that only goods moved easily. People were also highly mobile. When Phileas Fogg decided to circumscribe the globe in eighty days, he could leave on the spot, carrying English pounds—no passport, no visas, no problem with currencies. Never before and never since was so much of the world open to unrestricted travel, at least by a white gentleman. But there was not only the ease of travel for business or pleasure. For the first and last time in European history, perhaps in world history, masses of otherwise sedentary people migrated by choice, without being driven from their homes. Just as the private businessman maximized his profit in the market, immigrants maximized with their feet, moving toward better opportunities. Some, it is true, fled famine, persecution, or hopeless economic stagnation, but the Irish, the Russian Jews, and the Calabrians were not the only emigrants to the Americas and the white dominions. In the very countries where growth was most successful, England, Germany, Scandinavia, each crisis or setback generated a wave of migrants, and there was a steady flow even when times were good at home or depressed abroad.

We must pause for a moment and analyze this flow. We are now wrapped up in fancy theories of growth, capital formation, development, and technical progress. Yet here is a case we can explain with the simplest of classical models. In Europe there was little land per worker, and wages were low. In Canada, the United States, Argentina, there was much land, and wages were higher. True, the difference could be reduced by having the Europeans crowd into local factories and eat the food they "produced" by selling cloth and shoes for products grown across the ocean. But many preferred the direct way and simply went to join the highly paid American farmers. Perhaps they came for liberty as well as income, but the noneconomic aspects were not all positive. It was difficult to leave the landscapes, the language, the customs of home, even if countrymen and relatives beckoned from "over there."

The movement of goods and people also involved the flow of capital. This is a far more mysterious flow, for there were no piles of capital on harbor docks, no great liners full of capital steaming past the Statue of Liberty. Capital exports from Europe meant loans and shares. Production overseas, or in Eastern Europe, was developed with funds advanced by the more developed nations. Before goods could be produced, machinery had to be imported, buildings, railroads, and docks had to be built, and commercial networks organized. Europeans lent the necessary people and goods, and received securities entitling them to a share in the future profits of these enterprises. Because rich resources were waiting to be developed and also because such distant ventures entailed high risks, the returns were attractive to European savers. Some have argued that growth in Europe was held back by the outflow of capital, that the machines and other resources invested abroad would have improved productivity at home. But there were real gains from capital exports too. When overseas production increased, raw materials came into Europe more cheaply and more manufactures could be sold to the enriched markets abroad.

To be sure, some of the prosperity was fragile. If the less-developed countries borrowed to buy consumer goods or war materiel rather than to develop their productive capacity, they had no way of paying off the loans, except by borrowing more. When World War I came, with its political upheavals in Eastern Europe, many of the borrowers defaulted on their loans. One can argue that the returns had been high enough to take this risk into account, but nevertheless international lending acquired a bad name in the 1920s. Since then, the international flow of capital has regained importance, though with greater limitations on the type of loans available, especially to backward countries. In Part III we shall examine the decline and revival of international mobility, and shall be able to understand, if not always to share, the nostalgia for the pre-1914 era as a golden age of one economic world.

Mobility was not confined to international movements, of course. Within each country movement had become legally free and technically easy. Great factories produced for the whole national market, and the brand name replaced the local, word-of-mouth reputation of producers. Capital was also free-flowing, thanks to a complex system of banks and other financial institutions. A merchant in Hamburg might borrow from a Frankfurt bank that drew on new deposits by someone else in Berlin—or even in Hamburg! But the most visible movement was that of people to towns and cities. Birth rates were falling, now that children not only survived more often but demanded longer education and upkeep. The result was, for the first time in centuries, a real decline in the population of rural areas.

The cities absorbed huge amounts of investment, for apartment and office buildings, for new streets and public facilities, and for the public transport systems that tried to keep ahead of growing congestion. It must be said that the engineers of late nineteenth-century Europe were better than the architects. They stuck to a functional approach that has worn well, whereas the decorative flights of fancy that cover the public buildings especially did not mark an improvement over the earlier classical or baroque architecture.

There was a negative side to the great national and international mobility of the time. Economic crises and depressions now spread quickly, leaping regional boundaries and national borders. When a bank failed in Vienna, the rumble was heard around the world, and times could be bad from Chicago to Naples. The great leverage provided by specialization and mobility could work in reverse too. Everyone's job now depended on many incomes, many sources of goods and finance. The "pyramid of credit" was an especially vulnerable point: banks lent large fractions of their deposits, and lent for a long time. If a big customer defaulted, and especially if depositors began to worry, there would be a "run" on the bank. Then would come a cascade of runs and defaults, as everyone suddenly found his creditors clamoring and his debtors deaf. Sometimes, but not always, central banks or great syndicates of private houses moved in massively to attempt to reverse the trend and reestablish confidence. If they failed to move quickly enough or in adequate amounts, chimneys stopped smoking and goods lay idle in shops and warehouses because men had lost the income with which to buy.

This was depression, the frustrating sight of poverty amidst plenty. Marxists saw it as proof of the fundamental contradiction in capitalism. Traditionalists talked of over-production and of the sorcerer's apprentice. Bankers called for discipline and confidence, and populists murmured darkly about "malefactors of great wealth." It would take until after World War II to sort out most of the answer, an economic answer. The road to stability lay through two main policy changes. One was the provision, by govern-ments, of backup financial institutions to stop panics and eventually to prevent them altogether. This also implied control over private financial practices, so that there would be a minimum of recourse to the guarantees. The other change, even more far-reaching, involved control, again by the government, of the over-all volume of economic activity, so that there would always be a close balance between the total supply of goods and the total demand for them. This macroeconomic balance, intellectually worked out by J. M. Keynes in his classic *General Theory*[10] of 1936, still left room for the market to match the demand and supply for *particu-lar* goods. Indeed, Keynes saw his contribution as the way to save the market system from the shock of violent cyclical fluctuations.

At the same time as Europe was expanding its trade and becoming more concerned with managing the turbulent stream of economic goods, there was also a renewed rush toward political control—with or without direct annexation —of those underdeveloped, non-European countries still remaining more or less independent. From about 1870 to World War I, the Great Powers rushed in to snap up every-thing that was not already tied down. It was, without doubt,

[10] J. M. Keynes, *The General Theory of Employment, Interest, and Money* (New York: Harcourt, Brace & World, 1964).

an unsavory show. No amount of talk about the *mission civilisatrice,* as the French called the "white man's burden," could disguise the total disregard for the "natives." But was the motivation economic? This is a famous debate, and we have agreed not to become enmeshed in famous debates.[11] We can boldly and baldly say that imperialism, especially in the form of formal takeover, was not mainly economic, and concede that the point is still moot.[12]

Now that capitalism, however modified, has survived a half century since World War I, it is fairly clear that colonial markets are not its mainstay. Even in the late nineteenth century, the most promising road to growth lay in the new technologies rather than in attempts to lock up yet more distant markets for one's textiles and mass-produced housewares. Admittedly, many individuals and firms made excellent profits out of colonial trade, and exclusive possession of influence brought further profit to the European over the locals; for weak, high-cost industries or for shady and speculative traders, such markets were in fact necessary. But the real question is how these people managed to have such an impact on European public opinion and governments. I would suggest that the new imperialism provided a relatively safe outlet for nationalistic passions, the tensions of power politics, and the military buildup that went with them. Economic justifications, like the professed paternalistic motives, were no more than accessories. Both were useful, precisely because they were in some measure real.

[11] Lenin was the foremost advocate of the neo-Marxist thesis that imperialism, along with war and monopoly, represented a violent (and vain) effort by the mature capitalist system to escape collapse. Today, a more diffuse feeling that the advanced countries, consciously or not, deal unfairly with underdeveloped ones is widely prevalent. In fact, the drastic repercussions on poor economies of changes originating elsewhere result also from their backwardness and the accompanying rigidity and instability. When rich countries sneeze, poor ones catch pneumonia. The development strategies of underdeveloped nations must balance the dangers of openness with the almost indispensable advantages of being able to exchange goods, men, capital, and knowledge with other economies.

[12] See p. 154 for a discussion of the more significant, informal kind of imperialism.

Finally, it must be granted that the nature of international economic relations made for increasing political interference. So long as trade was mainly in goods, it mattered little whether the trading partner was a protectorate or not. But when one's investors controlled the railroads, the plantations, and the banks in such a territory, they demanded protection against expropriation and discriminatory taxation, or simply against the abolition of special privileges. This problem is not, alas, any less acute today, as the Cuban case shows. And it has a particularly vicious dynamic: the longer and harder foreign control is maintained, the more likely it is that the reaction will justify the worst fears of the investor. Furthermore, the foreign enterprise, even when it is progressive and desirous of contributing to the local economy, tends to find itself almost automatically allied with the most privileged and conservative segments of a stratified society.

In the first decade of the twentieth century, however, these problems seemed minor ones, easily handled by a few gunboats or King's Rifles. Nor were Europeans fully aware that their own system was rapidly changing from within.

One important trend was in the pace and nature of technological change. Up to then, new techniques had relied little on science, and they had often been tied to the development of new resources. From the 1860s, if such a complex change can be dated, resources were to fade in importance, and science to grow. The era of cheap transport and effective communication, of new materials and really cheap goods, was beginning. With capital, technical manpower, and managerial skill men could produce almost anything in quantity, or could find an effective and cheaper substitute for it. Scarce coal could be replaced with oil or hydroelectric power, or could be brought from a distance. If land was scarce, food could be grown more intensively, preserved, stored, and transported at will. But why elaborate, when the results are so well known? The economic gain, which is less obvious, consisted in new dimensions of mobility and control. Not only could resources move, they could easily be shifted to entirely new uses or could be redeployed in more favorable combinations.

The new technology required firms to look further ahead, since they now had to invest resources not only in buildings and equipment, but also in laboratories, pilot plans, technical personnel, and prototypes. Until the new product or process was found, developed, and commercialized, no payout came from all this expenditure. Partly for this reason and partly because the results of any one research project were uncertain, firms tried hard to achieve security in their market position and greater diversity of output and markets. In this period the first industrial giants emerged, but even size was not enough. Firms also joined together in a variety of agreements and mergers, ranging from price fixing in specific products to the formation of giant trusts, uniting whole industrial sectors and reaching across national boundaries.

The attitude of the great firms toward governments was ambiguous. On the one hand, businessmen still remembered the shackles of regulation and interference whose removal had done so much to promote expansion and development. Laissez faire was the religion of business, particularly in Britain and the United States, but elsewhere as well. On the other hand, commerce and industry made many demands on governments. Sometimes they sought protection from foreign competition or organized labor, or special privileges and a favorable colonial foreign policy. But they also, and more legitimately, were beginning to look to governments for economic stability and education, the two great requirements for implementing the possibilities opened up by scientific progress. Unfortunately, the distinctions between constructive public action and interference, between legitimate demands and privilege, were not always carefully made either by businessmen or by their critics. Even today, people tend to take an unhelpfully dogmatic approach toward the economic role of government, although we shall see, in Part III, how a more pragmatic attitude in this respect has contributed to the fine economic performance of Europe since 1945.

Thus, the second great economic change in Europe, as the nineteenth century wore on, was a potentially far more active role played by governments. Whether this was for good or ill remains an unsolved, and historically insoluble, question. Those on either side can point to successes and failures, forecast doom or utopia, and contrast their own ideal with the other man's reality. In the next chapter, we shall examine the objectives of public economic policies and consider briefly whether the state is the enemy of the market or its ally. As historians, however, we must emphasize specific means and concrete results rather than ideal aims and might-have-beens. Since 1914, government has *in fact* come to play a much greater role in the economic life of industrial countries. Our interest is in the many reasons that explain this fact and in the methods and consequences of public action, again in the perspective of economic growth.

We have been looking ahead, however. To the inhabitants of the *Proud Tower,* as Barbara Tuchman calls Europe before 1914, socialism meant no more than crackpot intellectuals, labor unions, and perhaps barricades and anarchist bombs. Despite growing international tension, social unrest, and economic crises, Europeans took for granted the pillars of their economic world: the gold standard, cosmopolitan trade and finance, private property, and the continued primacy of industrial Europe—wealthy, productive, enterprising, powerful, and articulate.

PART III

EUROPE
SINCE 1914

CHAPTER 15

Introduction:
Government
in Economic Life

The nineteenth century had seen a tremendous development of productive power in the economies of Europe. By
1914, few if any ultimate *technical* limits stood in the way of
economic growth. We need hardly recall the bases on which
the system rested: free markets, free enterprise, private
property. These provided the incentives: the carrot to har-
ness the skill and imagination of entrepreneurs and the
stick to ensure that workers stuck to their drudgery. They
also made possible, if not painless, the rational allocation
and reallocation of resources in response to changing tastes,
improved techniques, and new sources of materials.

Yet we have noted a series of problems facing the potentially affluent society. National rivalries led to political tensions, arms races, and military confrontations. Within nations men rebelled at the ugliness and brutality of industrial
society, and at the contradictions revealed by extremes
of wealth (and poverty), and by economic cycles or crises.
Less obviously, the market either ignored or dealt haphaz-

ardly with many economic problems, such as those posed by urban crowding and the need for education. Furthermore, the most vocal champions of laissez faire were often least disposed to permit uncontrolled markets to function in fact: whether in industry or trade, they used the advantages of size and wealth to stabilize, and also to bend, the price mechanism. They favored competition and free trade with one small exception—their own market!

The economic difficulties of advanced economies—war, social equity, stability, monopoly—all had one common trait. Their solution tended to limit the market system and to reinforce those who looked to the government for a more active role. In the latecomers to industrial strength, such as Japan, Russia, and to some extent Germany, the state had from the start taken an active part in the development process, so that less readjustment was required.

In trying to compress the turbulent events and patterns of a half century into a few pages, in Part III we will focus on the role of government in economic life.

The theory of prices and resource allocation assigns a subordinate role to government in a market economy. The government is supposed to keep order, provide a few general services, arbitrate and interpret legal differences, and manage money—but to intervene in the market only marginally or in exceptional cases. The pressure for greater intervention has, however, proved very great.

Pressure arose first because of the complex of issues posed by what can be called public business—that is, economic activity not undertaken in response to market signals, yet deemed necessary. Maintaining order and defending the nation against military attack are classic examples, but education, road building, and river valley development illustrate the scope of the issue.

The essence of public business is that a service cannot adequately be paid for by those who benefit, as the distribution of benefits is difficult to determine. The service is therefore impossible to price and must be provided by society as a whole, working through the government. This obviously in-

volves taxation, since providing benefits without charging
for them implies charging some of the people for services
they do not receive. How are the taxes to be levied? Here we
introduce the second function of active government, income
redistribution. Although many feel that redistribution is
not a legitimate use of political power, men have insisted on
using the political power to tax in order to modify the man-
ner in which the market distributes wealth and income.
Ideally, it would be good to separate the two functions of
taxation—financing public expenditure and changing relative incomes, but this is impossible.

Another function that government has increasingly assumed is that of stabilizing the economy. Originally, in the
market economies, the role of government was limited to
control of money. The symbol of value and unit of economic account obviously needed the full protection of political authority, lest lack of confidence in its steady value
bring chaos. The difficulty was that the guardian himself
often spent the monetary reserve to finance public business,
and thus subverted the value system placed under his supervision. It is not pure chance that central banks in France
and England were private organizations, under government
supervision, rather than arms of the state. Yet with the passage of time, and even in mercantilist days, financiers and
ministers realized that there was more to money than keeping it "sound." Monetary adequacy or its lack contributed
to general prosperity or stagnation. Later, in industrial Europe, the vexing phenomenon of the business cycle increasingly became an object of concern, especially when the
quality of the harvest ceased to be the determining factor in
business and price fluctuations.

For a time, men felt that monetary mistakes, particularly
lack of discipline in issuing paper money, were alone responsible for cyclical disturbances, and that the job of governments was to avoid laxity in their own business and to
restrain speculative excesses in the private sector. We have
seen how crises resulted in the late nineteenth century from
chain reactions begun by the failure of some speculative

venture or from panic induced by doubts about the sound-
ness of banks and companies. It took the painful experience
of successive crashes and depressions to teach men that one
could not artificially segregate government finance, the
banking sector, and the rest of the economy. Stability was
not achievable if each sector tried to keep its house in order
with no concern for the others, since the corrective measures
taken by one could increase the difficulties of another.
There had to be an equilibrium of the whole, with an imbalance in the government budget, say, to counteract an opposite discrepancy in private spending, or with the banks
taking risks to carry firms in difficulties long enough to
avoid a cumulative process of fear and crash. Thus taxes—
and government expenditure—have the additional function
of regulating the total volume of activity in the economy.

Stability of the price level, and of economic activity in
general, is also closely tied in with the equity problem we
have mentioned in discussing taxation. In times of buoy-
ancy, usually with rising prices, it is best to be an entrepreneur, that is, a borrower. It is not bad to be a wage earner,
for jobs are plentiful and wage demands not vigorously contested. But to be a retired employee on a pension, or a *ren-
tier,* living on fixed income from securities or real property
(that is, to be a lender), can be perilous. When times are
bad, and prices stable or falling, the shoe is on the other
foot, except that the situation is probably worse on balance,
since resources are lying idle instead of turning out goods.

The rate of change of prices, however, is probably more
important than the direction of change. One can argue
about the respective merits of mild inflation and somewhat
less buoyant stability, but sharp inflations and deep depressions have no economic advantages. When in addition they
succeed each other in sharp bursts, things are at their worst.
Economically, the great loser is investment, the tying up of
income in productive capacity for the future. Capital formation is sacrificed in favor of unproductive hoarding, speculative trading in inventories, immediate after-me-the-deluge
consumption, or the search for a foreign haven by those who

happen to be profiting from the immediate situation. Socially and politically, interest groups form into warring factions held together by the menace or the experience of ruin. Again and again, in interwar Europe, social cohesion would break from the strain of such movements in the economy. The end result could be an authoritarian takeover, as in Germany and Italy, or numb stagnation, as in France.

Problems of stability have frequently been aggravated by international complications, both commercial and financial. Often, the first drastic effect of an imbalance shows up in the balance of payments. When prices rise too sharply in one country, foreigners stop buying there while their own goods find an easy market. Or, if trouble of another kind is in view, capital leaves the country in speculative haste, so that everyone wants to sell the local currency and claim foreign money. No market can function if everyone wants to sell and no one to buy, and the currency cannot, therefore, maintain its value. In addition, incipient depression at home leads to calls for keeping foreign goods off a market already unable to take the domestic goods offered it. This means higher tariffs, but a variety of more drastic measures are available or can be devised to strengthen the protective effect. We shall follow the cumulative unraveling of the great international network of trade and financial connections in the interwar period. For a time, however, capital remained too mobile, leading to drastic pressures on a sequence of currencies.

We have by no means exhausted the catalogue of reasons for government intervention. There is the special problem of war and reconstruction, when the proportion of total output devoted to "public business" becomes so large that the nonmarket tail wags the market dog. Then, regulation and direct allocation are the rule of economic life, not its exception. Excess incomes are prevented from bidding for scarce goods: They are taxed or borrowed away. Patriotism, either spontaneous or enforced, becomes the dominant motive for economic action, replacing the profit motive at least to an extent. Yet war profits show that it may be efficient to supplement patriotism with a little selfishness, and also that suspending the market system leads to inconsistencies and opportunities for those who obey economic laws in preference to political ones when they conflict.

In fact, one of the great institutional innovations of the twentieth century in Europe has been the black market. Although not without its sinister and cruel aspects, it should not simply be relegated to some economic chamber of horrors with the slave trade and child labor. The black market was a natural outgrowth of the breakdown of legal markets. It provided, in particular, for the many cases in which the attempt to replace market signals with regulation led to absurd situations. In Europe, during the immediate postwar period, it was usually impossible to be in a regular situation with respect to all the laws and rulings officially in force. So, reasoned the war- and depression-seasoned Europeans, as well be hung for a sheep as for a lamb, and they set up what came to be known more genteelly as "parallel" markets.[1]

Government interference obviously tends to feed on itself. Every price signal it distorts leads to further distortions and to responses requiring additional measures. Even the goals are often at variance or at least interact strongly. Measures to improve the general economic structure affect the stability of the whole, while stabilizing steps lead to political pressure or to foreign repercussions. Indeed, this is perhaps the weightiest argument of laissez-faire champions, who would rather suffer the ills they have than risk enmeshing the economy in a series of well-meaning, but increasingly chaotic, measures of economic policy.

This is a telling argument, but Europe, at least, has now overwhelmingly rejected it. Concern for stability is one im-

---

[1] Planned economies, such as that of the Soviet Union, are also faced with the impossibility of providing for all the economic situations that may arise. In addition to ordinary black markets, resulting from general scarcities and rigged prices, such economies also depend on specialists in inconsistencies, who quietly bring together extra (and unplanned) demand and supply in the industrial sector, with at least the tacit permission of the authorities.

portant consideration. Another is the interference with the freedom of markets by the participants rather than by the state itself: nationally and internationally, many markets have been dominated by one or a few sellers, or sometimes by a few buyers, who could influence the price and thus distort relative incomes as well as the structure and volume of activity. How effective they have been, in view of market forces limiting their action, and whether governments have the political will and the economic skill to counteract their action in the public interest, are hotly debated questions. Public control at least limits the extent to which market power can be exploited by those who possess it, although it may, by distorting and weakening the action of markets, provide more opportunity for restrictive behavior.

Yet in the last analysis, the major reason for an increasingly active government lies in the importance of what we have called public business, and in particular the collective adventure of national economic growth. In the backward countries, and in Soviet Russia especially, development through centralized direction of the economy has been a conscious objective. In Western Europe, on the other hand, governments backed into this role at a later stage. They found themselves deeply enmeshed in regulation, and even ownership, of enterprises as the result of depression, war, and the need to mobilize resources for reconstruction. After World War II, when recovery was carried forward into real expansion beyond prewar levels, governments directed to the new task the vast powers they had accumulated, complementing the efforts of an invigorated private sector.

This brings us to the final problem, that of planning. It is strange that so innocuous a term, expressing the most basic qualities of organization and prudence in any endeavor, should have acquired such fiery connotations. Here, planning is the magic ingredient of any economic policy worthy of the name; there, it is anathema, the symbol of subversion and ruin. It is well to clear the air right now. The issue is not, today and in practice, between laissez faire and a planned economy making no use of markets. It is between two forms of mixed economy, both involving considerable government activity in production, consumption, regulation, and welfare. Without planning, the different aspects of government action remain uncoordinated, so that measures are taken without much concern for their impact on other aspects of policy or on the economy as a whole. Planning simply aids these elements, permitting conscious policy choices in terms of alternative possibilities and also contingency measures to cope with unexpected developments.

Indeed, we need not call it planning, if the word is unacceptable; nor need there be a Planning Commission or Board. Yet, it is easier to bring all the public and parapublic bodies together if we have an explicit mechanism to do so and if we provide enough authority to overcome the particularist instincts of entrenched programs and organizations. The state may find it possible, and even necessary, to carry out economic policies without admitting that laissez faire is no longer appropriate, but the job is hard enough without such a charade.

Finally, planning carries dangers, of course. It brings out clearly the costs of a given policy or course of action, and may thus crystallize the opposition of those most directly affected. This has occurred with labor unions and other groups in postwar France, for example. Planning can also turn errors of forecasting into major disasters by enlisting much greater resources in one (mistaken) direction than would otherwise be the case. At the end of World War II, for example, the advanced countries, particularly the United States, were still obsessed with the fear of depression, when in fact the major characteristic of succeeding years was inflation based on high demand. If planning had met the threat of unemployment by prompt expansionary measures, the postwar recovery might have ended in monetary chaos and a repetition of interwar crises.

Despite its economic dangers and despite the greater danger of political totalitarianism posed by an economically active and powerful government, public action will continue to control or influence a large share of the economic process.

In that case, it may as well be planned as left in the haphazard state determined by the accidental origin of so many government programs. Of course, planning, by making public action more effective, may lead to a Parkinsonian mushrooming at the expense of private activity. But it can also allow the necessary jobs to be done with a *minimum* of resources, reveal mistakes and omissions, and provide the clarity necessary for democratic control of a complex web of activities. The essence of action outside the market is precisely the absence of market signals, in the form of prices. Since they are absent, or incomplete, they must be complemented by planning.

In the East, where the market system has been rejected for its reliance on private ownership of capital, the problem is the opposite—how to remove the ideological bias against the use of prices and market incentives, and how to reconcile the existing plan with greater reliance on automatic mechanisms of response to market signals. The symmetry is striking, and the similarity between the two economic systems ever greater. One can only hope that both can and will use their success and the attenuation of their rivalry to combine in helping with the pressing problems of the underdeveloped world. Yet before allowing ourselves to contemplate this rosy vision of Europe's economy in the 1970s, we must return to the trials and turmoils of the past half century, to the twenty years of crisis and the twenty years of growth before and after World War II.

CHAPTER 16

The Interwar Period:
Aberration
or Apocalypse?

The economic history of the two decades between World Wars I and II is usually discussed in terms of economic policy. In many ways this focus is ironic, since governments were so little able to control events and fluctuations that the very term policy is hardly applicable, connoting as it does some idea of purpose and direction. Even when the measures taken were followed by improvement, it was often for the wrong reasons or at least in highly unexpected ways. Clearly, forces were at work with which neither the private nor the public sector of the economy could cope. Yet in a sense it is appropriate to focus on economic policy, since the mistakes made, and the inadequate or wrong analyses, were an important factor contributing to the continued difficulties. No wonder, then, that laissez faire found its most ardent and articulate champions precisely during the period when the capitalist system appeared to be exploding from the strains of its own contradictions. These apologists saw that the interventionist cures were sometimes worse than the disease. In addition, the succession of crises and inadequate policy responses severely retarded economic growth based on improvements in technology, organizational knowledge, and economic understanding. In all fairness, we must admit that crisis and war proved powerful, if painful, stimuli to the development and implementation of new ideas.

There are many ways of viewing the interwar period in the longer perspective of European economic history. One possibility is to see the twenty years as a troubled interlude in the general process of development, an interlude marked by a series of shocks aggravated by economic ignorance and amplified by political unrest exploiting the difficulties. In this view, the postwar period of growth merely resumes the advance of the nineteenth century. A contrasting approach is that of the Marxists, in which the crises and depressions are seen as marking the death throes of the capitalist system. Its collapse had been delayed first by imperialism and then by war. Only more war, and later more exploitation of (neo-) colonial peoples, would make possible the recovery of the late 1930s and of the postwar period. Although this is somewhat baldly stated, it is the point of view underlying the common emphasis on international big business as the key manipulator of economic life in the twentieth century.

Finally, one can see the period as a transition, a particularly difficult one, from one type of development to another. The fundamental changes are those suggested in Chapter 15. One aspect of the transition concerns the stepped-up pace of technological change on the basis of the systematic use of science. Not only has science been applied to changing techniques, but the whole process of scientific and technical investigation and management has been made systematic by the development of generalized tools such as statistics, measurement techniques, operations research, and computers. A second fundamental aspect is the increased interdependence of economic life, translated by a new scope for government activity. Here the problem is one of integrating public action with the market, so that the freedom, initiative, and efficiency of a decentralized system can be retained. On this showing, the war of 1914–1918 can be viewed as a complicating factor, but one not directly caused by economic forces. Economic ignorance also enters into the explanation of the troubled interwar years, but with the qualification that the problems faced, both by the private sector and by policy makers, were novel and truly complex.

We need not insist on the profound shock that World War I represented for Europe. Money figures as to its cost, of dubious accuracy at best, only satisfy the craving for something tangible without providing any real illumination. Human losses are more intelligible. The dead numbered 12 million for Europe, including 2 million Germans and 1.4 million Frenchmen. But one must double these figures to take into account the deficit in births due to the war, and must also add the high mortality from epidemics and malnutrition immediately afterward. Finally, many of the wounded and gassed were severely handicapped, and it must be remembered that most of the dead were young adult males, the backbone of the labor force.

Materially speaking, we must keep some perspective in viewing the effects of the war, now that we have World War II as a comparative measure. Of all the major powers, excepting Russia, which essentially seceded from the European economy, only France and Belgium had suffered any real loss of productive capacity. Yet the war on balance helped even the French economy, whose capacity to invest had previously been underutilized. To be sure, the capital stock in all countries had aged, as there had been little replacement. But productive capacity may well have been higher over all in 1919 than in 1914. Nor should one get confused on the subject of debt. The Allies owed considerable sums to the United States, and the Germans were faced with potentially heavy reparations, but most of the war had been paid for internally and by real surplus *currently* produced. The "grandchildren" were mainly in debt to one another within each country. They would not, as a group, have to pay for their elders' war.

With this perspective, we can perhaps evaluate more soberly the course of events after the war. Europe had every reason to regain her prewar economic strength, in terms of total production. Nor, as it turns out, was the basic Versailles scheme economically unworkable. This called for German subsidy of the European Allies, who would then be able to reimburse the United States for its loans. It would mean, however, a continuation of the exceptional conditions of war economies. Let us see why this is so. For one thing, it would require solidarity among allies, and between former enemies as well. Germans had to work so French and English factories could burn their coal, while the Allies would draw no net benefit, since they had to send goods to America in payment for war loans. The United States, on the other hand, would be required to accept heavy net imports (or else to forgive the debts). Self-interest working through markets could not accomplish such transfers.

There was more, however. Although productive capacity was adequate, Europe's industrial structure would have to be greatly changed to manage a collective effort of reconstruction and renewed peacetime growth. Not only did countries have to produce for one another more than before the war, but the nature of overseas markets had changed. Industrially speaking, the United States had come of age, and a number of other nations had begun serious industrialization in the absence of European goods—and competition. To sell abroad, Europe had to develop the newer sectors. England, especially, felt the full weight of her previous lag in transforming her industry. The world market would simply not take much cloth and textile machinery, while English coal production was by now inefficient.

Such a wholesale transfer of resources would have necessitated the retention and further extension of pervasive national and international government interference in economic life. In wartime, resources are allocated by decision rather than by the structure of relative prices. It would have been necessary to plan the international economy in terms of reparations and other transfers, and to assign each partner targets for specific goods to be made or bought.

The model for a post-Versailles settlement in fact exists. It is provided by the postwar experience of Eastern Europe, imperfect as the Soviet-dominated trade system has been since 1945.

All this is speculation, however. No such system was set up, and management of the Versailles settlement proved hopeless by monetary means alone. The overriding concern of all countries was to return to "normalcy;" most of them viewed international transfers as merely an aid to that accomplishment, and neglected the problems that such transfers would pose for the world economy.

The French wished to return to their semi-isolation, counting on reparations to keep them financially strong without the necessity of any fundamental economic transformation. The United States simply wanted to be rid of European involvement, with the proviso that there should be no leftover debts. The United Kingdom was more sensible about financial matters, since the British had the largest stake in restoring the lively trade and capital flows of the prewar Pax Britannica, but their error was in thinking that the economy at home would take care of itself if only prudent and disciplined financial management prevailed. The Germans, finally, preoccupied with the consequences of the breakdown of Imperial order, had no very clear thoughts beyond a general unwillingness to pay the kind of reparations envisaged by the French, who in turn saw the matter as a straightforward squaring of accounts from 1870, with interest.

During the first years after the war, generalized inflation infected most national economies. This was due in part to high demand for resources for reconstruction, but mostly it brought out in the open the repressed price rises of wartime. In France and in Germany, there was, it must be said, little incentive to financial discipline. The French government found its internal debt much easier to manage with a depreciated currency; the Germans knew that the amount of reparations would be increased if they seemed well-off, while inflation and even chaos could be laid at the door of unreasonable Allied claims. Yet both countries made considerable economic progress in these years. In Germany, this was all the more surprising, as the mark completely lost its value in a hyperinflation and France occupied the Ruhr for a time, threatening to paralyze German industry completely.

Great Britain, on the other hand, went at the currency problem first, and pursued a deflationary policy from 1921 on, but especially after 1925. The British were prepared to limit investment in order to reestablish the pound sterling, and with it the financial primacy of London. The government was also willing to face labor unrest, culminating in the general strike of 1926 just after the pound was reestablished at its prewar parity with respect to the dollar. The heroic gesture of "normalcy" ignored, or tried to efface, the much greater inflation of English prices relative to American ones due to the war.

But it was a misguided gesture for more fundamental reasons. With the breakdown of the international economy, progressively in the 1920s and even more in the 1930s, even a fully healthy pound would have been less profitable in terms of international trade and finance than it was before. Therefore, the game was really not worth the candle. And the economic cost was too high. Britain was forced to keep the level of activity very low to bring domestic prices down, and this reduced the level of investment below what was necessary to achieve the modernization that had already been tardy before the war. Finally, the overvalued pound was of little use as a practical asset, despite its brave facade: international capital was well aware of the discrepancy between the rate of exchange and the real value of the pound, and soon looked for a safer denomination in which to keep funds.[2]

This brings us to the subject of currency crises and capital

[2] A disturbing, if imperfect, parallel can be drawn between the 1920s and the 1960s. In both cases Britain has put short-run stability before growth, each time to stave off a fall in the value of the pound, and each time unsuccessfully.

movements in the interwar period. We have already encountered international financial flows in discussing the nineteeth century. These were the vehicles of exchange in goods and ideas and the means by which development tended to spread from the European centers. Most of the capital flows of the interwar period were of a different nature. The capital was like bank deposits, highly liquid and highly mobile. To the extent that it moved in response to higher yields, reflecting lively demand for funds in one place, it was useful. But international short-term capital was also highly responsive to any doubts about the stability of a currency. If there was any danger of the pound depreciating, it fled London, say for Paris, only to seek a surer haven if the franc seemed in danger. In turn, of course, any flight of capital away from a currency greatly reinforced its incipient weakness. One can say that the rats gnawed holes in the side of the ship as they left. Although similar mechanisms had been at work in the financial crises of the prewar, now it was an entire national currency that was threatened and not merely one bank.

The other factor in currency questions was the balance of trade, that is, the difference between exports and imports. Because of inflation, reconstruction needs, and the deterioration of free trade, many countries found themselves in balance of payments difficulties (of which the United States seemed to be the chronic beneficiary). In order to remedy this situation and to provide a sound financial environment attractive to international capital, governments resorted to deflation. But this usually led to political and social strife and to a weakened economy, in turn scaring off the jittery international investors. Finally, a good deal of highly speculative domestic activity took hold, either due to euphoria, as in the American stock market, or to desperate attempts to right a precarious position. Such speculation reinforced the instability of international financial movements, as well as sharpening the hostility of left-wing and middle-class groups to liberal capitalism.

Nonetheless, from 1926 to 1929 it seemed as if Europe

might be over the worst. The pound had survived restoration of its prewar price. The franc was also stabilizing, although at a far lower value, and the French economy was more active than it had been since the 1850s. The German mark, a brand new one after the total debacle of hyperinflation, was being supported by American capital, so that Germany could pursue its reorganization of the economy, concentrating enterprises, investing in construction and new equipment, and improving urban services. In Britain, unemployment was declining. And at the periphery of Europe, as well as in the United States, things were on the upgrade. Italy had settled down, after considerable anarchy and violence, to its peculiar experiment in state guidance under Mussolini. Russian communism looked less fierce in these days of the New Economic Policy. And across the seas, as we know, the United States was enjoying the liveliest boom in its history. Automobiles, movies, the radio, the airplane, all seemed to promise plenty of investment opportunities for industry for many years.

Then, after 1929, the economic world of the West collapsed. The world crisis was triggered in the United States, by the stock market, but soon spread to Europe, and the resultant depression held the stage until drowned out by the thunder of war. In its essence, the crisis was no different from others in the period: a financial collapse spreading among countries and followed by a decline in production and trade. But it was sharper, deeper, more widespread, and more lasting than earlier crises. Furthermore, it ended for good any hope of restoring the international "normalcy" of prewar days. The solutions eventually found in various countries were all resolutely national, as we shall see. And when, after World War II, the international economy again began to function, national priorities remained what the thirties had made them: first a viable and balanced domestic economy, then international trade and capital flow.

The world crisis had a number of immediate causes, and

there were also fundamental weaknesses in the international economy contributing to its severity. Whether these considerations add up to a satisfactory explanation is another matter. Without question, governments did not react to minimize the impact of economic trouble either at home or in other nations. To some extent this nonaction was due to economic ignorance, especially of the fundamental Keynesian factors making for stability. After all, Keynes' *General Theory* came out only in 1936, so that even immediate application of its lessons would have helped little. Yet the problems went beyond what Keynes' model envisaged, for the book applied essentially to a closed economy, whereas the crisis was emphatically an international one, propagated and deepened by negative developments in foreign trade and finance.

The immediate causes relate largely to vulnerable financial positions in the various countries. In the United States, which we must include here, the well-known orgy of speculation in the stock market was reinforced by excessive consumer purchases on credit, with everybody's spending based on the inflated paper value of securities. Great Britain clung to its overvalued currency and its reliance on trade in a world where nations were turning inward. Germany had a double problem. Much of its temporary prosperity depended on American funds that could be recalled at short notice, as indeed some were as early as 1928 to feed the hungry boom on Wall Street. Moreover, we have seen that German banks made very full use of their power to create credit; in particular, they tied up in long-term loans to industry funds that could be claimed at short notice by depositors. Although this contributed to development in stable times, it made the financial system, and the economy with it, highly vulnerable to shocks.

France was in a different position. Her currency had not been definitely stabilized until 1928, and then at a low value that cushioned it from further depreciation, in addition to lowering French prices. Her trade did well, therefore, and capital began to flow into Paris. For this reason, the crisis hit France last, and in a way least, but no single European country could remain unaffected in the long run, except perhaps peripheral ones such as Italy and the Soviet Union. Yet their cases are also interesting, because they previewed what the rest would soon do in response to depression, namely, find a national and nearly self-sufficient solution, no matter how inferior to the idealized free and open economy the others talked of but could not recapture.

The fundamental factors making for depression are somewhat harder to evaluate, since they may have been the result of events as well as the cause. But Europe did face a series of unfavorable changes relative to the period before 1914. Domestically, the growth of markets was slowed by a general fall in birth rates. This in itself is not necessarily depressing, but where population grew, the expansion was due to continuing increases in longevity, which meant an ever older population. This in turn reduced the demand for housing and other goods depending on family formation, and it undoubtedly dragged down mobility and willingness to innovate.

Abroad, as already mentioned, World War I had led to great increases in productive capacity and output. World prices of commodities fell in the 1920s, leading to widespread agricultural depression well ahead of the general world crisis. Yet the increase in primary production overseas did not provide more markets for European manufactures— since prices fell, the incomes of agricultural and mineral producers failed to keep pace, while their own industries fought to withhold from former European suppliers the markets captured during the war.

Between 1931 and 1934, the European countries abandoned hope for any quick general solution to the international crisis, and each set out to put together some sort of viable national economy. The particular solutions depended on the political conditions prevailing, on economic circumstances, and probably also on differing national styles. There was almost always a gap between announced intentions and actual performance, but we have seen that governments faced new tasks poorly prepared and informed, and that the private sector still reeled from the shock of economic reverses and contradictory policies. Ideological conflicts and international tension added to the gloom and apprehension, without stimulating (except in Germany, alas) any renewal of energy or cooperation. Yet, in the midst of confusion and hostility were being sown the seeds of the new economic system that has developed in the postwar period: a mixed economy in which the state takes considerable responsibility for economic growth and stability, and for the distribution of national production.

Today's mixed economies have incorporated two currents that figured in the patched-together systems of the 1930s. One is, of course, socialism, in the sense of public control or public ownership of productive resources. We should note, however, that neither regulation nor nationalization was usually the result of conscious socialistic impulses. Instead, government intervention grew out of wars and crises, and there was rather more of it in Nazi Germany and Fascist Italy than elsewhere. Nationalization usually resulted from financial trouble in important enterprises, such as utilities and railroads. Only the partial nationalization of the Bank of France came in response to political demands for a check on malevolent high finance.

The other current, far less clear in its doctrine, is corporatism. This also represents an attempt to control or bypass the market mechanism. It relies on the explicit organization of economic sectors and interest groups into bodies such as chambers of commerce, regional or industry associations, unions, and other groups. The novelty is to give such bodies real powers in setting economic policy and in controlling markets, either directly or through their association with government agencies.[3]

[3] The short-lived experiment with the NRA in the United States was, for better or for worse, part of the mainstream of the ideology of corporatism.

Corporatism was an important ingredient of the fascist system, if it can be called a system, although the function of the corporatist structure was in fact to facilitate control of the economy by the government. Yet in the years since World War II much of this impulse has remained and has been turned to more constructive uses. The French modernization commissions in the planning mechanism are a case in point: representatives from various firms in an industry meet with government officials, sometimes also with union representatives, to discuss the growth of their sector in relation to the economy as a whole. Although such practices send shivers of horror up and down the spines of Anglo-Saxon believers in the virtue of impersonally competitive markets, there is little evidence that growth has suffered as a consequence. Nor should Americans, at least, feel too alienated by talk of corporatism, for the Washington lobbies and the various regulatory commissions of the government clearly encompass elements of the same system, and are perhaps more dangerous in that they are not officially recognized and therefore are not subject to close political control.

We now return to the 1930s, and will conclude our survey of the interwar years with a description of the different national solutions for coping with the collapse of the world economy. The chief interest of these expedients, in addition to innovations and premonitory signs of later practices, is in the interaction of economic measures and political events, and in the way the experience of the thirties shaped the objectives and preoccupations of European policy makers in the 1940s and 1950s. For we should not be misled by the magnitude and horror of World War II into thinking that the European nations were concerned only with effacing its terrible traces. There was no wish to return to the caricature of normalcy that had been the thirties. On the contrary, each nation was determined to remedy the grave faults in its economic life that had been shown up in the crisis. Britain, which came through the thirties and the war best, remained something of an exception, and as we shall see, was least disposed to change.

The 1920s had been harsh on Britain. We have seen the cost of financial pride, and have also noted the growing difficulty Britain faced in selling traditional exports to a world that had made great strides in industrial development. There had been severe labor trouble and continued unemployment. In 1931 the pressure finally proved too great. The two pillars of Victorian England crumbled when the parity of the pound and free trade were abandoned. As it happened, these two measures were followed by considerable improvement in the economy. No longer did domestic production have to be held down to accommodate a fickle international market, while free trade was replaced with a system of imperial preference that kept enough trade flowing between the United Kingdom and the Dominions to sustain home industry and feed the British population.

It was, like everywhere else, a second-best solution, but at least a viable one. Indeed, something of a real revival took place in Britain in the 1930s. The gap in newer industries, such as automobiles, electricity, and chemicals, began to be filled, while a great deal of house building brought unemployment down from some 22 percent of the labor force in 1932 to half that rate in 1937. It was not prosperity by any means, but it was something, and government regimentation and intervention were far less than elsewhere. Nor had the social consensus been shaken. The great political cause of the period was, after all, the love of Edward VIII for a divorced commoner.

The experience of France was in many ways the opposite. The French economy entered the crisis with a decade of relatively vigorous growth behind it and a strong currency. Until 1933, the economic storms swirled about her borders with little impact. Even when the crisis finally did bring depression to France, the number of unemployed never rose as high as a half million, compared to 1.8 million for Britain in the *recovery* year of 1937. The accuracy of the French figures is doubtful, it is true, but their order of magnitude is not.

Nevertheless, the depression had severe consequences in

terms of economic production as well as social conflict. For the bad times brought out most strongly the "Malthusian" character of the French economy, in the sense given to the term by the French. Although each enterprise, except for the few large ones, could cope well with adversity, the concern for distributive shares and the suspicion of others were exacerbated. By 1934, France was on the brink of civil war, despite the small number of unemployed and the relative self-sufficiency of the economy. The polarization of the body politic into Right and Left made effective government action impossible, although there was neither the competence nor the information in economic matters to have effected any fundamental changes even in the absence of political paralysis. After 1936, when the conflict had become dulled, production continued to stagnate almost completely. Despite considerable armament expenditure and a continuance of relatively high employment, one cannot really speak of economic recovery in prewar France.

In the other major countries, a much more consciously directed economy was in force during the 1930s, although only in Germany was this in direct reaction to the crisis. In order of increasingly drastic interference with the principles of the market, we shall look briefly at Italy, Nazi Germany, and the Soviet Union.

The fascist state of Italy under Mussolini had no coherent economic policy to go with the high-flown rhetoric of the regime. Public works were undertaken, it is true. Marshes were drained, good roads built, and the trains made to run on time, as all Europe noted in admiration or irony. Yet total productivity lagged, so that government investment and armament expenditure were paid for by a general fall in real incomes. The real contribution of the regime was in providing, unintentionally, an institutional framework for postwar growth. Large firms were encouraged, particularly in the modern industries, and they have permitted Italy to play a highly honorable role in the recent technological rejuvenation of Europe. In addition, the government was forced by its totalitarian aspirations to take ultimate responsibility for economic difficulties. During the 1930s it thus found itself controlling the banking system and taking over a considerable number of enterprises. Since 1945, the Italian government has had the leverage and the power to implement an active policy of high investment without neglecting stability and the major problem of regional development.

The National Socialist regime in Germany began with an avowed hostility toward large-scale capitalism and high finance. But the socialist element quickly faded before the nationalist one, and the regime found no difficulty in incorporating the existing economic structure into its scheme. For this reason, the economic system evolved under Hitler cannot be considered radically new. It preserved private property and markets, and only superimposed on them a complex network of control, planning, and corporatism. Full employment was quickly reestablished with the help of massive public programs of investment and rearmament. Total control of foreign trade and exchange prevented any check to activity because of possible balance of payments problems, while the difficulties of combining strong central direction with a market economy were also avoided. This last should not surprise us, despite the serious theoretical problems it poses. The softest democracies have easily managed the job in wartime, and the Nazi regime simply made the state of war a permanent condition. It was helped by the presence of convenient scapegoats accepted by many Germans: communism, the Jews, the Versailles Treaty, the confusion of the Weimar Republic; and, it must be said, by a widespread taste for order and authority. Yet no great reliance was placed on popular enthusiasm, which was complemented and shored up by the systematic and uninhibited use of terror.

The remarkable material success of the Nazi economy is easily understood. The Germans simply used resources fully, without political constraints on the amount of output the state could withhold from current consumption. In the United States, during World War II, the state also mobilized great numbers of men and huge quantities of goods, tolerated what seemed appalling waste, and still allowed higher civilian consumption than during the 1930s. Probably, much of the luxuriant bureaucratic apparatus of the Nazis was of little or no use—it made no difference. So long as there were no idle resources and no limitations on their allocation, growth could proceed. As we shall see in discussing the postwar Soviet Union, the problems arise when one tries to add a measure of freedom and choice as "goods."

In the 1930s, however, the Soviet Union vied with Germany in its totalitarianism, and far outdid it in the drastic nature of economic change. We have noted previously a kind of breathing spell there in the 1920s. All sizable industrial enterprises were in public hands, but farms were owned by peasants and private activity was even encouraged in trade, handicrafts, and small-scale industry. The noteworthy contrast with Czarist development resided in the policy of allowing peasants to consume most of their harvest or to sell it at remunerative prices. The Soviets thus hoped to encourage greater productivity. Nonetheless, the New Economic Policy placed them on the horns of a dilemma. If they wanted to resume rapid industrial development, they had to capture more agricultural produce. To use taxation, as the pre-Revolutionary regime had done, discouraged productivity. Yet an agriculture of small, owner-worked farms, in Russia as elsewhere, tended to result in well-fed farmers with little incentive to change their methods or sell much food. Nor were the Soviets willing to encourage a capitalist farming industry of *kulaks*.

A lively debate thus marked the late 1920s, while the Soviet Union made quiet progress and restored some of its economic ties with the West. In 1928, Stalin brusquely cut off debate with a solution more drastic and immediate than had been envisaged by any faction. It was the Czarist pattern, heavily reinforced and, it turned out, minus the former reliance on trade with the now-depressed West. Stalin ordered the collectivization of agricultural land, and, more importantly, coupled it with the first of a series of ambitious plans for industrialization. The Five-Year Plans emphasized heavy industry, there being no longer any need to coax food deliveries out of agriculture with consumer goods. Some machinery was imported, but the world market for wheat was poor and most food went to feed industrial workers rather than for exports. Industrial output grew rapidly, mostly in the forms of heavy equipment to produce materials, and machinery to produce heavy equipment and more machinery. There were no problems of markets or demand, nor much attention to costs of production.

Since industry managed to develop, collectivization apparently succeeded. The cost, however, was staggering. The peasants, especially in the rich Ukraine, resisted collectivization with all the despair their memory of serfdom and exploitative taxation aroused. Perhaps ten million people died in the process of forming the kolkhoz, or collective farms, and most of the livestock also died or were killed by unwilling peasants. For they knew what was coming. Not only did they lose the prized security of owning land, but the state again appropriated much of the crop with no real compensation. Before, it had been taxes, now it was a delivery quota paid for at confiscatory "official" prices. In time, the necessity for increasing food production led to some degree of compromise. The state provided agricultural machinery, allowed the peasants to work small private plots, and even permitted the sale of collectively grown crops beyond the quota at good prices in "free" markets. It was an oppressive system at best, run by party politicians instead of agricultural technicians, but it was no longer virtual war with the city-centered state.

Like Germany, the Soviet Union under Stalin showed that rapid industrial development and economic growth were possible with little reliance on foreign trade. The Soviets had to overcome greater handicaps, since their stock of "human capital," in the form of an industrial labor force and a trained body of technicians and managers, was critically small. Yet it could be managed if human and political values were discounted entirely. We must, however, make a distinction between the two cases. In contrast to Germany, Russia had known nothing but oppression and poverty and now there was at least long-range hope for real economic betterment and social justice. This probably sustained the population through hardship and political terror more than did actual fear of the authorities. The great purges of the 1930s thus appear to have been gratuitous as well as bloody.

This, then, was the European economy in the late 1930s: a set of closed-off, largely antagonistic, national units, each trying to recapture the momentum of growth in its own way. It was a discouraging picture. The "gathering storm" of war, even when its full consequences were not foreseen, gave scope only to the most negative kind of expansionary government policies in the form of arms buildups. Moreover, the democracies were clearly most shaken by depression. Their governments acted hesitatingly at home and seemed paralyzed in their foreign policy. Understandably, there was much talk, even among non-Marxists, of inherent stagnation or instability under capitalism. The fruits of science, the opportunity of new techniques, the adventure of enterprise and mass affluence, all seemed a hollow mockery when resources lay idle next to bread lines. It truly seemed that only dictatorships could make the wheels turn again, and many were half-ready to swallow the gibberish of propaganda, the artificial grandeur, and even the brutal terror, just to get their society off dead center. Then came the war. The need to strike down the monstrous growth of fascism soon banished any thought of this as an acceptable framework for full employment and stable growth. Europe would have to find another way.

CHAPTER 17

The Postwar
Resurgence of the
European Economies

It requires a major effort of perspective and choice to tackle the economic history of Europe in the last quarter century. Too many names and dates crowd our memories, fed largely by the news media, and it is easy to turn the story into a kind of alphabet soup of economic institutions flavored with the diary of solemn international agreements and confrontations. On the other hand, we must also avoid presenting a catalogue of current economic problems in industrial countries. So we shall focus resolutely on the problems and successes of economic growth since 1945, seen in the perspective of interwar failures. For the postwar period has been dominated by growth, most notably in the efficiency with which economic resources combine to produce goods and services, in short, by greater productivity.

That World War II—nearly six years of it in Europe— was costly, needs no particular emphasis. It combined the deadliness to the fighting man of World War I with an incidence on civilian populations that Europe had not experienced since the Thirty Years' War of the seventeenth century. Material destruction was on an unprecedented scale as well, although the loss of productive capacity proved less severe than had been feared. Wartime Germany provided the first clue to the resilience of the industrial apparatus, when it was realized that production had been affected surprisingly little by the mass bombings of industrial cities. Housing proved a more lasting problem, but housing shortages had only a limited effect on subsequent production.

Human losses were something else, although Western Europe, on which we are focusing attention, got off lightly compared to the Slavic countries, Germany being an exception. It is safe to say that few people—the depression of the thirties still fresh in all minds—worried about a coming scarcity of labor. Yet it has turned out that a chronic labor shortage has in fact threatened to muzzle growth since the mid-1950s, what with the losses of the war and the previous demographic slump.

Despite bombings and dismantlings, and despite the absence of replacement and maintenance, Europe's capital stock was far from eliminated. It needed repair and reconstruction, but this was much cheaper than recreating the whole from scratch. One rebuilt bridge, for example, reopened a whole section of railroad or road. On the other hand, the very extent of destruction provided the opportunity to make great improvements in quality and suitability in the process of restoring the capital stock. The latest machines could be installed, layouts made more rational, obsolete installations left unrestored with no regrets. In addition—and this proved of great importance—an invisible stock of capital remained in the form of skills, education, and working habits embodied in the people of Europe. Human capital perhaps more than anything else, even massive American aid or the will to recover, explains the speed of reconstruction and renewed growth. It also accounts in large measure for the contrast between the various "miracles" of Europe and the painfully jerky progress of non-European underdeveloped countries.

It would be unjust as well as misleading to minimize the difficulties of reconstruction, the hardships and sacrifices that war-weary people still had to face before material conditions became less harsh and drab. Nor can one ignore the contribution of the United States, less because it was generous than by contrast with the shortsighted and hurried exit of 1920.

But the fundamental change that occurred was Europe's regained capacity for growth. In each country the mode of growth was conditioned by preoccupations reaching back to the 1930s.

For France, there was no question of going back to the prewar period. Whatever the charms of slow and civilized change, the failure to grow rapidly had eventually resulted in total stagnation, in near-civil war, and in the galling and ignominious collapse of 1940. The essential fragility of the French compromise with development had been shown up. The future could only lie in the spirit of the Resistance, combining action, unity, and courageous honesty. In fact, change would not prove so drastic nor so pure, but its pace did accelerate markedly.

There was one immediate and practical development. As a result of slow change and low birth rates, France had been managed and guided by old men, of whom Marshall Pétain was a symbol. These men were largely discredited, and replaced by much younger people in positions of responsibility, the younger in that World War I had taken so heavy a toll of the intermediate generation. For the next twelve years, a quiet but far-reaching change was wrought in both the private and the public sectors of the economy, a change largely overlooked in the midst of financial and labor troubles, bloody colonial disengagement, and French involvement in the Cold War. In this change the "new men" played a great part.

England emerged from the war with relatively light visible losses and high morale, but having become the debtor rather than the creditor of its dominions and colonies. Its capital stock was largely intact but badly in need of renewal. Yet there seemed to be little realization that the long-term international viability of the British economy depended on a major technological and managerial renewal. Instead, the British were conscious of the need to limit consumption in order to free goods for exports and avoid price increases, and at the same time were concerned that the burdens should be equally, or at least fairly, shared. In fact, economic equity was the foremost consideration. It guided the policies of the Labor government, which carried out nationalizations, raised taxes on high incomes and luxuries, and instituted social welfare programs as comprehensive as anywhere in the capitalist world, equalling Sweden.

The difficulty was that investment and enterprise suffered. There was little government action in the traditional sphere of the private sector, industrial production, while the economic policies introduced provided the wrong set of incentives. Existing disparities of *wealth,* with their peculiar British social concomitants, were not materially disturbed. But punitively progressive taxation of *income* made it scarcely worthwhile trying to better one's earnings, to put forth greater effort, or to take risks. The benefits of public housing and comprehensive health insurance were for all, indeed especially for the less well-off. The combination of limited opportunity, a secure minimum, and ten years of austerity triggered a consumption boom, from the early 1950s on, that has since repeatedly threatened the stability of the economy and the pound. We shall see later how this has contributed to a rate of growth almost uniquely low for Europe.

Germany, on the other hand, knew how to grow, as had been demonstrated repeatedly. Her fundamental problem was to reconcile good economic performance with democracy, the openness and diversity of Weimar with the efficiency of Bismark or Hitler. This is in fact the German miracle, not the revival of her ruined cities and torn-up industrial plant. Democracy and decentralization coupled with growth are the real achievement behind the slogan of a "social market economy."

Yet, for the first three years after the collapse, Germany waited in a paralyzed economic vacuum for a clear indication of Allied policy. There was talk of measures far more drastic than dreamed of in the *Diktat* of Versailles, and the Allies, particularly the hard-hit French and Russians, were already dismantling factories. It was also clear that a harsh settlement, if one were agreed on, would this time be enforced directly by the armed might of the occupying powers. Passive resistance or a show of helpless inflation would do no good. So Germany waited, her economy a Kafkaesque parody of a modern industrial system. There was almost no legal activity, although here and there the most frivolous and secondary articles were turned out because they were too insignificant to be regulated by the thorough Nazi system, which was taken over, almost intact, by the occupying powers. One could not even say that prices were high. Money was simply irrelevant, transactions being by means of barter or through the new medium of exchange, cigarettes.

Gradually, and confusedly, the tide turned. It was clear that the Americans, who called the tune, had no stomach for creating an industrial vacuum in Germany, if only because it would require their continued military control there indefinitely. The break with the Soviet Union made the new policy definite and hastened its application. Germany, or its western part, would be included in the Marshall Plan and be built up as part of a democratic Europe. German authorities were gradually put in supervised charge of the three western zones, and they moved to lift the paralysis by restoring a real currency.

Monetary reform sealed the ruin of those who had relied on financial holdings or on pensions, but it brought the economy to life. There had been goods on hand, although not many, but no one was willing to sell them for money until assured that the money would buy other goods. Now firms *had* to sell, since they had no other source of funds to finance new production. The revival gathered speed in a changed climate, and there was no looking back.

We can deal more quickly with Italy and the Soviet

Union. The Italians faced less inner conflict than the Germans, for their dictatorship had provided only the semblance of order and growth. But they, like the French, also had to find the key to sustained growth. With the help of abundant manpower, apparently such a handicap, and of American aid, they managed to fuse democracy, capitalism, and the institutions of fascist *dirigisme* into a powerful, if not always orderly, engine of growth. The Soviet Union, on the other hand, simply took up where it had left off in 1941. Its industrialization was not, after all, so different from war, even in its toll of lives. We in the affluent West must wonder at the patience and perseverance of the Soviet people, unwearied by fifteen years of hardship and police control, undiscouraged by the terrible losses of war, prepared to continue with the handicap of a large permanent military establishment. They may not have chosen the policy of forced growth, but they put up with it and gave their best efforts. The reparations taken from Germany and from several East European satellites were only of incidental help, painful as their transfer may have been for the "donors."

Western Europe, then, undertook the task of reconstruction from war with the thought that people had to look beyond the immediate and obvious objectives to a workable system for the longer run. It is in this perspective that we can evaluate the role of foreign, particularly American, aid. For the two gravest dangers faced by all the nations of Western Europe were, on the one hand, social conflicts, in this case revolt on the part of organized labor with Communist backing, and on the other, balance of payments crises leading to sharply nationalistic and neomercantilistic reactions, as in the thirties. Foreign aid allowed governments to relieve some of the pressure from the desperately low levels of consumption, and also to finance the beginnings of social welfare programs which tempered worker anxieties. Because the balance of payments was protected by dollar aid, governments could avoid resorting to the kind of restrictive manipulation of their currency and prices that had marked the twenties in England and the thirties in France.

Public expenditure for reconstruction and new investment could go on, with access to the imported food and
equipment that were needed immediately. For aid represented not only more resources, necessary to supplement the
feeble productivity of war-torn economies, but also a much
wider choice of goods than could be mobilized within the
country in the short run. Even if it had been possible to
restrict consumption more, there would have been no way
to build immediately the fertilizer plants and rolling mills,
the mining machinery and earth-moving equipment that
were necessary to pursue recovery.

The United States did more than make it unnecessary for
each country to rely only on itself. It actively encouraged
intra-European trade, and thus set in motion a gradually
increasing current of trade and specialization that came to
have a considerable impact on growth. In the beginning,
however, most of the imports came from the United States
(and Canada). With them came more than food and industrial materials. Europe had fallen sharply behind the New
World in terms of technology and management, and the flow
of ideas and methods from west to east was perhaps as important as that of goods. Machinery incorporated the latest
improvements, whether in continuous-strip rolling mills or
catalytic cracking units, and there was also active human
exchange, as in the productivity teams of the Marshall Plan.
The American business religion of efficiency through constant change struck a responsive note among Europeans in
search of a new impulse for growth.

Sometime between the beginning and the end of massive
American aid, Europe turned a corner. At the beginning of
the 1950s, businessmen and governments were still preoccupied with shortages and restrictions that made ordinary
affairs far more complex than they should have been, and
there were also new problems. World raw material prices
rose sharply as a result of American rearmament and stock-
piling following the beginning of fighting in Korea. The

industrial countries of Europe felt the pressure of higher import prices, and the French were even forced into a mild recession. Yet in the midst of day-to-day or short-run problems, these same businessmen and public officials, and the farmers and austerity-wearied workers too, were launching Western Europe on a unique binge of economic growth, less and less concerned with making up war losses. All the indices of output and consumption passed the levels of 1938, then the high-water mark of 1929, and kept rising.

What was the character of this sustained wave of growth?

First of all, to emphasize the point, the major element was the improvement in efficiency of resource use. Most of the countries were limited in their ability to add productive resources. Only Italy and Germany had a reservoir of unemployed labor to absorb, and they used the opportunity to grow even faster than the rest. Investment reached and sustained high levels: the European countries were investing something like a quarter of their total output, and it was difficult to withhold more than this from current consumption. But new techniques and better organization, coupled with entrepreneurial aggressiveness and public encouragement, led to impressive progress.

Numbers are misleading, and growth rates more than most. On the one hand, rapid growth at first was normal, given the low *levels* of the immediate postwar period. On the other hand, while it is hard to get excited over an annual rate of 4 or 5 percent for total output (GNP), we must recognize that this did represent substantially better performance than the 2-to-3 percent considered honorable in the century of European development.

Because productivity improved and real costs fell, the economies could run at full employment and increase levels of consumption without sacrificing financial stability. This factor was important, for a delicate equilibrium on both the material and the psychological levels had to be maintained. Full employment was good in that it meant full use of resources, while reasonable price stability was also necessary, particularly when trade was liberalized. But the memory of depressions and currency crises also lingered, making even the possibility of unemployment or inflation politically and economically dangerous. This did not mean that Italy resorbed her unemployed immediately, nor did it prevent the French from running periodic sustained price rises, but everyone had to take into account the sensitivity that existed toward disequilibrium. A mild degree of inflation, which can be called upward price drift, in practice proved the best compromise: it allowed full employment and favored borrowing (for investment) by lowering the real value of the capital at repayment.

Stability and competitiveness through productivity growth were increasingly important as nations cautiously opened their borders to freer trade. This, however, was only one of the ways in which trade contributed to sustaining and accelerating growth. Many of the technological possibilities that became available to Europe required a far larger market than any single country. Adam Smith was vindicated all over again, as trade led to specialization and the benefits of large-scale production. These benefits were especially great when there was a major effort of research and development to finance. Not only could firms amortize this over a larger volume of sales, but the limited stock of R&D potential in each country could be concentrated on a smaller number of projects and products. The result has been that capital goods, embodying improvements in production technology, have been more and more actively traded as the users of production equipment looked abroad for the wherewithal to remain competitive. No one country could hope to keep up in all the kinds of equipment being developed.

Another result of trade has been to increase greatly the amount of competition faced by producers. Small countries, and by the standards of today's mechanized and specialized industrial production the European countries are all small, have always faced the dilemma of competition versus scale. The former requires many firms, the latter few. Only with trade can the two be reconciled. There may be the additional advantage that it is harder to achieve monopolistic collusion internationally than among members of one national industry, although the believers in international cartels will argue that one should not underestimate the cooperative talents of businessmen. At any rate, the generalized commitment to active, if less than entirely free, trade has severely limited the ability of firms and industries to seek relief from foreign competition through tariffs and other barriers, although it has not ended their pleas.

The private sector has learned to accept and expect a more constructive kind of government help. Such help has taken many forms, from formal plans, as is the case in France, to a situation where the government "doth protest too much" its respect for the market economy, as is the case in Germany. In fact, the real impact of government in all areas has been considerable, if not always well-advised.

What does the government provide? First, it has stressed everywhere that economic growth with stability is a primary and serious objective of public policy. This means continued high levels of demand, tempered, however, by the need to maintain the value of the currency. As a consequence, private investors face a minimum of insecurity regarding the general prospects for business. They still lack the full assurance that government will have the skill and the means to handle all contingencies, but the techniques of monetary and fiscal management and of short-term forecasting have been substantially improved.

But the informational aspects of government action are not limited to global levels of activity. Here we may take the French planning system as an example, though it is only the most formal and articulated of many. In *le plan* (the successive French Plans of Modernization and Equipment), the expansion of particular industrial sectors is charted within the framework of growth for the whole economy. It is not clear whether the figures represent targets or predictions, but they are at least reasonably consistent with other planned developments in the economy, particularly when public action is involved. It remains true that the government does not take full responsibility for errors, in that private firms still have to sell their goods in the market, but the planners have a stake in securing the cooperation of industry, and a serious dedication to making the plan realistic as well as socially constructive.

Finally—and without this there would be little in European experience that offered any lessons for the United States—there is considerable direct public action. The government obviously builds, staffs, and operates what economists now call *social overhead capital:* the schools, the roads, the ports, and virtually all utilities and public transport facilities, so important in densely populated areas. But there is also a considerable nationalized sector of industry, while the financial sector is at the very least supervised by the central bank, and often largely nationalized as well. Thus, when French planners (or Italian regional developers) provide for specific measures, they are expressing far more than pious hopes. While the direct orders they can give are of course limited, they have a whole panoply of instruments, from "suggestions" for nationalized enterprises to tax advantages, public investments, and favorable loans for private firms. Such planning is basically a way of coordinating the multifaceted public sector in the interests of growth and then shaping the decisions of the private sector toward the same objective.

Between reconstruction, investment, and social welfare, the government has handled a high proportion of total output in all European countries. These resources have been used primarily for investment, although there has also been redistribution to the lowest income groups, those who are forced to consume all their income. On the whole, Europeans have become used to relying on government and on corporate profits (which remain largely undistributed) for the funds needed to increase productive capacity. Since the government, or similar agencies, has also largely taken over the task of providing for extraordinary expenses such as illness, education, and retirement, people have been free to spend their income. With the discovery of installment buy-

ing—the "never-never" as the British have called it—this
has meant a lively market for consumer goods.[4]

At first, Europeans used higher incomes to eat better, to
replace their overused wardrobes, and to enjoy the bright
lights that had been dimmed for so long. But in the early
1950s a great change took place. Europe discovered durable
goods, American style. The boom began with radios and bi-
cycles, expanded to motor scooters and vacuum cleaners,
and has now reached the full panoply of standard appli-
ances, television and phonograph equipment, and, last but
far from least, automobiles. The only real competitor for
consumer expenditures has been travel, foreign travel in
particular. The American tourist is no longer the bread-and-
butter customer of the hotel industry, despite the increasing
flow across the Atlantic.

It is true that the importance of durable goods industries
has made consumer spending a bit less stable in Europe,
since it is relatively easy to defer such purchases, but durables have provided great scope for technical progress. Not
only have costs, and even prices, fallen steadily, but consumer durables have "carried" a good deal of research and
development in metallurgy, chemistry, electronics, and
other growing sectors.

From this sketch of the general characteristics of European growth, one central problem emerges, that of inflationary pressure. Virtually everything we have mentioned,
except the growing volume of trade, contributed to a high
level of demand for resources—from shopping sprees to the
ambitious government plans, not to mention colonial wars,
foreign aid (given), and subsidies to agriculture. Trade
played a dual role. Comparative advantage means that imports cost less, in terms of the resources embodied in exports,
than would be required to replace them at home. This factor was important in Europe, as was the competitive stimu-

---

[4] There has, of course, been some private saving in Western Europe,
chiefly for the purpose of buying housing.

lus from abroad. Yet external conditions, lying outside the control of governments, often complicated the management of macroeconomic balance, while the need to remain competitive made inflation even harder to tolerate. For example, the Suez crisis of late 1956, which raised the price of the crude oil that Europe imports in huge amounts, completely swamped the already tenuous stability of the overextended French economy. Furthermore, the reaction of 1958 tended to be all the sharper there as it coincided with a lowering of French barriers to trade in relation with the first stages of the Common Market.

Inflation, therefore, was the key problem of the 1950s. This was fortunate for the Continental countries, since they were not yet fully aware of Keynes, and it turned out that his teachings, directly applicable to situations of insufficient demand, needed refinement to be useful as inflation fighters. Britain alone had learned the lessons of her distinguished son—learned them too well, in fact. Her governments again and again applied the Keynesian brakes. But these pressed hardest on investment, thus imparting a downward bias to British productivity and turning short-run overheating into chronically higher costs.

The Continental countries found other solutions, perhaps harsher in the short run, but less subversive of growth. France, politically hampered and externally burdened, simply allowed residential construction to lag until 1955 at least. Such a policy meant nagging hardship, especially for new families, but it was not an unmixed misfortune. In addition to freeing resources for more rapidly and directly productive investments, it slowed down, at least, the flood of migrants toward Paris, and also allowed France to emerge relatively unscathed in appearance from a particularly uninspired architectural decade.

Germany and Italy went at the problem more directly. They simply held wages down. The German labor unions were highly cooperative, to put it mildly, and stood by while an extraordinary fraction of the national income went to profits. It is true that reinvestment of profit income was high, but the disparity in incomes and wealth, which was accepted calmly during the "economic miracle" in Germany, would have shocked political opinion elsewhere. There was no such passivity in Italy, but labor could apply little pressure for higher wages so long as the South retained its virtual army of unemployed, or almost unemployed, labor. Only in recent years has the growth of the economy, coupled with foreign demand for Italian labor, largely dried up this elastic source.

In the later 1950s, the northern countries began to suffer from a severe shortage of labor, and stable growth was only sustained with the help of a uniquely massive stream of temporary migrants from the surplus countries of the Mediterranean. Qualitatively, the flow was nothing new. France had always found it difficult to recruit men for mining, construction, and other heavy jobs. If a Frenchman was willing to do heavy physical work, he preferred to do it in his own fields; so Italians, Spaniards, Poles, and later Algerians were brought in. Similarly, England had her Irish laborers, Prussia her Polish farm workers, and pre-1914 Vienna a polyglot host of menials from the many provinces of the Empire. But in the 1950s the phenomenon took on a new numerical importance. By the mid-1960s, one out of three jobs in Switzerland was held by a foreigner, the same Switzerland that has traditionally been so wary of immigrants in its position as the stable oasis in turbulent Europe. Greeks, Portuguese, and Turks joined the Spaniards and Italians of the first wave, notably in Germany. France and Britain relied more on non-Europeans from ex-colonial areas with which they retained "special ties."

Migrant labor has proved to be an economic godsend to the employing countries, and a welcome source of income, employment, and training to the less developed source nations, but the complex of social issues raised by such a large flow is far from easy to circumscribe. It can be said that Europe has been surprised at the smoothness with which it has been managed, given the cultural shocks, the artificial living conditions, and the built-in instability of such movements.[5] There is now a general feeling that it is prudent to limit the numbers of migrants involved, a conclusion reinforced by the somewhat narrower gap now subsisting between "Northern" and "Southern" countries in terms of demand for labor and wage levels.

In summary, we can say that the general, and healthy, response to inflationary pressure, when the demand for resources is potentially greater than the supply at existing prices, has been to increase the latter. Britain alone has tended to limit demand more of the time. But in fact, the British problem has been due to her assymetric response to the two kinds of imbalance. Excess demand has been countered by measures which in effect, if not in intention, limited investment, while the policy response to a slacker situation has taken the form of more freedom for consumers to spend. Because investment takes time, the burst of spending without previous expansion of the productive apparatus has spilled over into imports, thus putting immediate renewed pressure on the balance of payments, in any case the vulnerable point of so open an economy.

To conclude our survey, we shall try to delineate some of the special features of the various countries, especially as regards economic policy. This will give us a chance at least to mention the socialist group, whose growth performance has also been very impressive, particularly in view of its previous backwardness.

Great Britain has already been dealt with, at some length, if not kindly. I would draw a reasonably close analogy with the France of earlier days. The device on the banner of the nineteenth-century French "industrial revolution" was, if our previous analysis is near the mark, something like *"Qualité, Stabilité, Tranquillité."* In the pursuit of these ideals

5 Not to mention the recent memories of deportees to Nazi labor camps and of Displaced Persons.

the French sacrificed growth to an extent that finally made a mockery of their objectives. In a more affluent age, the British have sought the liberty of mild government intervention, the equality of a highly progressive income tax, and the fraternity of a comprehensive social welfare program. Yet, because they have sacrificed growth, they face instead constant public meddling to preserve precarious economic stability, the injustice of low social mobility, and the bitterness of labor in the face of unemployment and wage freeze. Recent analyses of the British economy have also noted a good deal of the "Malthusianism" familiar from our survey of prewar France: a hesitant attitude toward the new, coupled with sharp defensive reactions when established positions are threatened.

France has certainly not eliminated either social strife or the heavy hand of bureaucracy, nor has she transformed all her archaic and fragmented economy. But the negative aspects were known, indeed known too well, for they were still being analyzed at a time when a new capacity for growth had clearly been created.

Where to look for the key to the French revival? Obviously, once the climate of growth is present, many sectors behave more dynamically. Who are the leaders and who the followers—there is the question. One can focus on the role of the government, although real stimuli were also provided by the changed behavior of entrepreneurs, farmers, consumers, and the parents of larger families.

We have already mentioned the role of new men in postwar France. Among them was a group, loosely delimited, of young, highly trained, technically minded men who took positions of responsibility in both public bodies and private firms. They shared a common outlook, founded on their education, and were as close to one another as they were far removed from traditional French enterprises and politics. They have come to be known as the technocrats, and have been accused of, or credited with, a conspiracy to grow. Behind the smoke screen of technical complexity and the traditional autonomy of the French administrative system under weak governments, they supposedly threw out much of the apparatus of democratic bargaining and market competition on which the system was supposed to rest. They cared more, it is claimed, for the public interest than for any other, even that of the voters, shareholders, or elected officials whom they might represent.

There is something in this elitist view of recent French growth. It should not be exaggerated, for it does not explain increased birth rates, agricultural transformation, changed tastes among consumers, and many other aspects of growth. Nor does it deal fairly with the government, which has been wrong, obstructive, or sluggish much of the time and under both republics. Yet it is true, as so many cases have shown us, that too deliberate a weighing of the costs of change, too enlightened a vision into the near future, can paralyze action and make everyone worse off. In fact, one of the current problems faced by the French planners and policy makers is the erosion of their capacity to advance growth behind people's backs. International competition in a more integrated Europe is one factor, the other being the increased sophistication of interest groups and public opinion. The solution is to reintroduce democracy into the planning process, thereby committing powerful groups to the objectives and to their costs by reason of previous consent. So far, this approach has not been pushed by the Gaullist government, and it has been resisted by labor unions especially, for they have still felt too alienated and suspicious to abdicate their rights to protest later.

Every nation, especially when it is engaged in some great enterprise, appears to need its myths and slogans. We have seen that Germany has chosen to label its system a social market economy, in recognition of the fact that it achieves authoritarian efficiency with a large degree of decentralization and democracy. Yet it would be highly misleading to take the German protestations of economic liberalism at face value. What they mean is that the system is decentralized *for Germany,* and that the guiding hand of authority works subtly and with due regard for private interests and democratic forms. In fact, it would have been absurd that Germany, with so much public business in the form of reconstruction, refugee resettlement, and institutional restoration, have anything but an active government. In practice, the actual amount of government action has been limited by the contribution of other forms of coordination outside the impersonal market, although it remains true that few countries channel so high a proportion of their national income (some two-fifths) through government—this despite the comparatively modest costs of defense and other international affairs.

In Germany, the banks have played some of the role taken elsewhere by public bodies. In this, they continued the tradition of industrial control by which they had insured the safety and return of the capital they lent to industry. Because banks found themselves involved in several firms within an industry, they acted to coordinate growth within that industry, much as a French modernization commission might. There has also been a good deal of what would elsewhere be called planning, on the level of local and regional chambers of commerce and industrial associations. Such bodies have traditionally been more powerful than in Anglo-Saxon countries and more elitist than their French counterparts. They also have considerable legal status.

The government itself has promoted exports and other desirable activity, far beyond the proximate needs of reconstruction, and collected high taxes in the name of sound finance. It was free, almost until the 1960s, of any real pressure from labor. When this pressure began to increase, a more sophisticated and flexible economic policy was also developed, although it is ironic that so soundly managed and rich a nation should suddenly develop budget problems, as it did in 1966. Quite clearly, the margin for myth has diminished in Germany, and she now requires the full range of economic policy tools, including the despised anticyclical and planning measures, to deal with current issues.

The Italians have had less tendency than others to trumpet their growth as the result of some intellectual break-through, whether it be planning, the market, or some catchily named combination of the two. Yet their performance has been spectacularly good in the absolute, and so much better than that of the past that one has to restrain the impulse to label it miraculous. Too bad that it is the Austrians, another reputedly indolent people, who quip that they had the economic miracle, whereas the Germans were forced to work! In all seriousness, Italy has made virtues of her disadvantages. Weakness in coal and traditional industries has permitted the use of cheap imported petroleum and concentration on real growth sectors, from tourism to special steels from electric-arc furnaces. The presence of unemployment, as we have seen, eased the pressure on wages in addition to providing a kind of foreign aid to the Swiss and Germans. Even the stubborn lag of the Mezzogiorno, the backward South, has contributed to the success of the whole country. Since there was such difficulty in initiating and sustaining development in that region, only a limited amount of investment went south at a time when there were abundant opportunities elsewhere. And Italian agriculture did not absorb too many funds during the period of incentive-distorting wheat subsidies. Now that the country is better integrated with the wider European market, agriculture can focus on the products for which urban Northerners are prepared to pay: fruit, flowers, meat.

There are still two Italies, it is true. One is that of the North and the cities there: industrial, dynamic, European. Nowhere in Europe is there better design, more progressive technology, more aggressive enterprise. The other Italy is that of the South and the Islands, emerging painfully from near-feudal backwardness. It is reflected also in the bureaucratic lag of government and education, long the province of the less technical and managerial Southerners—the Church is not the only Roman institution trying to achieve its *aggiornamento*. All in all, however, modern Italy is a good object lesson to those who believe that natural resources or national character are primary explanatory factors in economic growth.

We are again neglecting the small countries of northwestern Europe, despite the many originalities and innovations in public policy for which they are responsible. They have all grown, although perhaps a bit less rapidly than the larger countries. No doubt, the smaller home market is a factor here, despite the high degree of specialization of all these economies. They have also retained a considerable degree of social cohesion, although linguistic and religious differences help maintain political activity, and even crises occur.

More interesting than the small northern social democracies (often in monarchic dress) are the southern countries, Spain, Greece, and Portugal. Without any major structural reforms, and particularly without popular regimes, they have had unprecedented economic growth. The sun and the past have proved to be valuable natural resources and "invisible" exports, while temporary emigration has also brought in foreign exchange along with heightened expectations and new ideas. The governments have managed to maintain a surprising degree of financial stability, although the slow growth of living standards for the mass of poor people, the apparent price for stable growth in these countries, has made social and political tensions at least latently more explosive.

We observe here a phenomenon familiar in underdeveloped countries today, but little known before. Growth relies on high profit incomes and it is also furthered by close contact with more advanced nations. Both factors, however, make poverty more difficult to tolerate even when progress is substantial and visible. There is an alternative path: closed development relying on ideology—and government investment—rather than on material incentives. Not without difficulties, this is the path followed by the socialist countries, at least until recently.

Indeed, it is probably in these incentives that we should see the main distinguishing characteristic of postwar devel-

opment in Eastern Europe. Clearly, the members of the
Comecon, or Soviet satellites, or Popular Democracies, as
one prefers, do not have a monopoly either on government
ownership or on planning and state control, although important differences of degree persist between East and West
in this regard. These countries entered the postwar period
with their small prewar potential devastated. They were
poor and badly underequipped in human as well as physical
capital.[6] It is comprehensible that they should have considered reliance on material incentives prohibitively expensive,
while the market mechanism had never shown strong signs
of bringing about rapid development and social progress.
This is not to suggest that Soviet-supervised communism,
with its heavy burden of political and bureaucratic control,
was either freely chosen or economically necessary. However, we cannot dismiss the basic ideas of limited association
with more freely consuming societies and of central direction as purely arbitrary ideological impositions.

In all of Eastern Europe, there has been rapid industrial
growth ever since the war. Doubtless, the highly centralized
system did not always make the optimal choices as to composition of output and methods, quantity often being put
before quality and too much attention paid to physical
amounts instead of values and costs. Once again, the appropriate analogy is a wartime economy, in which waste is normal and unavoidable as the price for speed. Over all, the
level of achievement is impressive. Even the considerable
human cost must be compared to the more distant past of
oppression and suffering with no growth or social leveling.
Industrial production has risen faster than private consumption in Eastern Europe, and social services have been
provided more readily than consumer goods. But in the socialist countries, too, people are beginning to pursue comfort and elegance and to enjoy durable consumer goods.

Yet all these countries, even East Germany, are still

6 The Soviet Union had transferred and increased its industrial plant,
while Czechoslovakia and East Germany resembled the Western nations.

largely agricultural. And this sector has been a much more difficult one to bend to socialist planning. The Soviet solution of collectivization was, of course, considered the normal model to be followed, and was in fact implemented. It has proved highly unpopular, however, and has fairly well been abandoned in the western tier of socialist countries. The Stalin solution of the early 1930s apparently proved too strong even for the authoritarian and doctrinaire regimes in power. In fact, the recalcitrance of agriculture to growth "by the numbers" has been a major factor in economic liberalization.[7]

Partial liberalization of agriculture has not solved all problems. In the Soviet Union, for example, the supplementary private incentives caused peasants to devote their best efforts to small plots farmed with little capital, while the collective fields were less carefully worked and the farm machinery was often neglected. Soviet agriculture did get a boost in the mid-1950s from large areas in western Siberia opened to cultivation. But, like the rest, socialist agriculture must in the main rely on improved productivity, which is incompatible with earlier practices of confiscatory prices and the management of agricultural units by party hacks instead of trained technicians.

In Western Europe, there has been greater reliance on price incentives to increase agricultural output, sometimes alternating with downward pressure on prices to force cost reduction. Of course, prices have not simply been set by governments, but the interference with markets has been persistent. The results of progress are evident everywhere. Even French agriculture has made up a large part of its lag, mechanizing and adopting fertilizers. While output has grown, productivity has done even better, for great numbers of European farmers have left the land for the cities or else have sought employment in local industry. Output has also

[7] The difficulties with agriculture have not been confined to Eastern Europe, and they explain, in particular, many of the failures of development outside the industrial countries.

shifted toward the kind of quality products responsible for
the established prosperity of countries like Denmark and
Holland, and suitable for a prosperous urban market.

There have been severe strains, however. Either food
prices have tended to be high, leading to inflationary pressure, or farm incomes have lagged, with political consequences exemplified by the blocking of roads with tractors
and produce. Then, too, the over-all progress masks great
unevenness. Much land is still fragmented, many farms are
still primitive. Finally, the human development of rural
areas has hardly been tackled, either in terms of raising production or of providing a fuller life for those who still remain incomplete participants in Europe's social and cultural, as well as economic, prosperity. The models are there,
and have been for a century—in rural cooperation and
credit, in folk high schools, and in extension services. But in
many areas, particularly in the South and the West, most
farmers do without them.

Economic growth has continued in Europe well into the
third postwar decade. The specters of depression and inflationary collapse have faded. Ideological dogmatism about
markets and government is also out of fashion, while there
is little talk of revolution, even far to the nominal left. Today's problems are those that preoccupy, or should preoccupy, Americans as well as Europeans. They are the consequence of affluence and crowding and of mass aspirations
for more than minimal standards of comfort, recreation,
and security. Some part of these needs can be filled by the
production of more goods, and would pose few problems if
it were not for the considerable resources taken up by the
remaining demands, and for recurrent checks on the growth
of consumption, especially of low-income groups, in the
name of stability particularly. Here we are concerned with
the remainder of the job. It can be summed up as the need
to provide a qualitatively better environment for economic
activity and for living. A nonexhaustive list of specifics in-

cludes education, for adults as well as for the young, urban
development, transport, regional and rural balance, natural
resource management, cultural activities, and health facilities.

It is not our purpose to belabor these well-known needs,
except to show their particular nature for Europe, especially
in contrast with the United States. Europe is both more
crowded and less wealthy, so that its inhabitants interact
more but have fewer resources with which to shape their
more critical environment. Moreover, Europe suffers from a
triple lag. The 1930s, and even more World War II, led to
great neglect of long-term improvements. Also, the postwar
period has seen a sharp demographic change. Previous war
and depression, coupled with higher birth rates since 1945,
have increased the proportion of the old and the young relative to those of peak working age (twenty-five to fifty-five).
Yet it is the latter who can build the environment, while the
dependent age groups make the greatest demands on its facilities. Finally, the very speed and suddenness of economic
growth have precipitated the demand for the environmental amenities of prosperity, at the same time as individuals have found it difficult to postpone immediate consumption so as to make resources available for the necessary investments.

Europe also faces some special problems in attacking the
job. While reluctance to entrust economic jobs to the government rises in America to the level of a prejudice, Europe
suffers from the opposite tendency to rely on the state for
anything falling outside the most ordinary production and
consumption of goods and personal services. It is true that
environmental investments have many characteristics of collective business, and therefore offer scope for public activity.
But there is a strong case for trying private, decentralized,
market methods first and where possible. There are many
pitfalls in taking a private "dollar" and putting it to public
uses without distortion and loss of efficiency (pitfalls largely
unconnected with any supposed dishonesty or incompetence
of public officials relative to others). Perhaps worse, how-

ever, reliance on the government for jobs in which there is no clearly optimal pattern of expenditure, but rather the need to innovate and use imagination, tends to diminish public concern for the specifics of environmental improvement and to deprive those left responsible of the diversity and vision of unofficial initiatives and thought. It must be said that the British, for all their supposed socialism, resemble the Americans more than the Continentals in this respect.

Much is being done. Every European city appears to harried motorists as one great construction site, and the newspapers are filled with news of reforms, plans, commissions, proposals, and analyses of deficiencies. Yet the political opposition insists that it is too little. In this field, it is necessary to run fast merely to stay in one place, and the job will test the vigor and stamina of an economically rejuvenated continent.

Our treatment of the twentieth century has given considerable emphasis to the role of governments, justified, I feel, by the historical evidence. To restore balance, we shall now look for a moment at a less-noticed postwar phenomenon, namely the rediscovery, or rehabilitation, of money and markets on both sides of the Iron Curtain—to retain the hackneyed term.

There is, of course, nothing new in the realization that highly open economies cannot permit themselves monetary looseness or severe distortions of the price structure. Indeed, the major difficulties of the interwar period came from the tension between domestic management of the economy and the requirements of financial discipline for international purposes. As we have seen, the eventual answer was to sacrifice the advantages of international specialization for better control at home. In the postwar years, the trend has been reversed, but governments have not found it easy to loosen their hold and to trade discretionary power for adherence to rules and market signals.

In the West, the first rediscovery was the importance of sound money and of balance in fiscal matters as well as in-

ternational payments. The Germans took to this idea first
and most readily, the Italians shortly thereafter, though
with little notice, and the French not until 1958. More
gradually, the virtues of free markets have gained increased
recognition again. It is not so much that the market mechanism is good in itself, as that it economizes the decision-
making and control capacity of public bodies. Its use wher-
ever possible allows them to concentrate on real policy
choices. To put it another way, political decisions require
bargaining, and are therefore inherently more costly than
impersonal and decentralized ones. For example, it has
often proved easier to induce mobility in people through
the forces of opportunity and competition than to secure
compliance with policies aimed at the same objective.

To the east, the advantages of market incentives over
commands, and of autonomy over central control in decision making, were first shown in agriculture, at least in the
negative sense that other approaches clearly did not work
well. More recently, with the most urgent shortages out of
the way, the concern for true economic efficiency has become
strong in industry. It is not enough, for example, to turn
out a great number of machines. The machines must also be
effective as well as efficiently made, thus economizing scarce
materials and skills in *use* as well as in production. This in
turn requires objectives much too finely detailed to be handled by instructions from a central plan, the more so as it is
necessary to control the achievement of targets as well as to
define them. It is far more efficient to let the users—consumers or other industrial units—control quality and value by
choosing what to buy. Yet this practice introduces the need
for appropriate prices, profit calculations, increased use of
money, and therefore over-all financial balance.

Another development in the socialist countries making
for greater attention to financial equilibrium is the cautious
opening up toward the West, now beginning to extend to
the exchange of persons. Yugoslavia, the pioneer in liberalization, has learned that there is too much incentive for illegal currency transactions when the national currency is not

reasonably valued and is severely controlled. As this is written, she is planning to make the dinar convertible in order to cope with the flood of tourists and of returning temporary emigrants. But the Soviet Union also worries about the extent of profit opportunities in illegal activity, as witness the severity with which "economic crimes" are punished, and the international incidents due to black market money-changing by foreigners. The lesson was learned in the first postwar years in the West, and later became acute in Latin America. Now it is being dealt with, hesitantly, in Eastern Europe, despite the same kind of prejudice against markets that long hampered Western nations with regard to public action.

CHAPTER 18 〜〜〜〜

Epilogue. Europe:
One, Two, or Many?

I f the public attention given to matters were a reliable in-
dex of their longer-run importance, there is no question
that "integration" would be the central fact of economic life
in postwar Europe. And indeed, we have emphasized the
extent and significance of renewed trade and mobility.
However, what is usually meant by economic integration, or
the building of "Europe," is a specific set of arrangements
between nations to increase contact within the group
formed, perhaps at the expense of its relations with others.
Most often stressed are such multilateral, and exclusive,
groupings as the European Economic Community (the
Common Market) or the Comecon to the east. This emphasis neglects bilateral agreements such as the economic union
between Belgium and Luxembourg, as well as numerous
limited arrangements for cooperation, particularly where
political lines cut across common interests. There are also
various looser groupings, such as the more "Atlantic" Or-

ganization for Economic Cooperation and Development that includes virtually all of Western Europe.

It is a serious mistake to begin and end every study of today's Europe with the particular institutional experiment known as the Common Market, and to evaluate all other intra-European relationships in its light. Interesting and apparently successful as it is, the Common Market leads us to forget two important points.

One is that there are many other levels of contact, exchange, and cooperation more limited or wider than this particular customs union. Within countries, the various regions, social groups, and branches of activity argue and bargain. Internationally, the same economic problems are reflected in myriad private and public relationships, often informal and even secret. Also, the split between East and West is becoming increasingly artificial as the ties within each bloc loosen and those between pieces of the two are multiplied. Formal reconciliation is difficult to achieve, more for political than economic reasons, but it does not prevent practical achievements.

The other point is more debatable, and will probably provoke the ire of dedicated "Europeans," who are not to be confused with Europeans. I suggest that unity is not the goal of European economic development in the postwar, but mainly a necessary means to it (or perhaps an incidental result!). One can, of course, argue that this is irrelevant, that governments are simply preparing their own (necessary) demise, while trying to promote national growth. But it is at least important to recognize the primacy of national objectives in government policy toward European matters. The French government under De Gaulle is far from unique in taking this point of view, and his originality lies chiefly in saying out loud what all governments have tended to leave implicit, or even to deny, while applying it in practice.

Our discussion of postwar growth has made it clear why mobility and cooperation are necessary to continued growth in Europe. The advantages of scale and specialization in the production of goods—and even more in the production of knowledge—as well as those of competition and financial discipline, need no restating here. We have also mentioned the value of matching resources, such as northern capital and southern labor, whether in the factories of Cologne or in Spanish real estate. Finally, it is clear that mobility is a consumer good as well as a productive asset in today's Europe. People like to travel, and it is impossible for large-scale tourism to exist in a neomercantilistic jungle of currency regulations, tariff barriers, and uncoordinated transport systems, as Eastern Europe is beginning to realize.

Perhaps if the national economies were nearly pure market systems, economic openness would not require any political relations beyond the civilities of diplomatic representation. With intervention at the national level, and with intergovernment action as a result of it, the political content of economic life also becomes international. For as soon as there is government intervention, there are political issues of priorities, burden-sharing, and income redistribution; these issues are political in the fundamental sense that there is no unique solution so rational that it makes everyone better off than does any other alternative. For German consumers to finance the investments of Italian and French farmers, or for taxes to be paid by the Dutch distributor rather than the Belgian manufacturer, may well be excellent economic measures, but they cannot on that account be adopted without political consideration of the total package of equivalences resulting from integration.

Economic integration is therefore a necessary part of continued growth, and it does lead to closer political ties. Yet the primary task of each government remains that of furthering the economic development of its own national community, and this goal is never lost sight of in the formation and implementation of international agreements. Nor should the view of European integration as based mainly on limited alliances with continued national sovereignty in essential matters be dismissed as obsolete nationalism. It is the welfare of individuals that matters, whether they live in a

"United States of Europe" or in a "Europe of States." National governments owe their considerable economic role to the collective trials of depression, war, and postwar reconstruction. To transfer the complex and highly political non-market functions of regulation, planning, redistribution, and collective action to some larger body would require a real international community such as does not today exist. For it has been clearly shown that all the cohesion built up within a national community by long cultural unity and shared experience is necessary to sustain growth under the mixed economic systems Europe knows today, particularly if totalitarian methods are to be avoided. As we have said, the priorities have been clearly established: national development will not be jeopardized either for the principle of a free international economy, as sometimes occurred in the nineteenth century, or for the more recent ideal of a united Europe.

Our conclusion, therefore, is that integration of the type exemplified by closed economic unions is only a part of a more general phenomenon of increased similarity and interdependence, affecting all Europe and extending beyond it, while it is itself restricted by the continued primacy of the national economy as the basic framework for solidarity and policy. There is little immediate likelihood of One Europe —or Two—for too many differences remain, in language and especially in "language:" the institutional, legal, and symbolic trappings of economic activity and policy. Nor should this be seen as unfortunate. Diversity has yielded a rich harvest of ideas, among others in the promotion of growth with stability and social responsibility. We can mention the French *plan,* the Yugoslav Workers' Councils, the Swedish *Ombudsman* (who protects citizens from bureaucratic injustice and insolence), and the first attempts at a planned progression of incomes in Holland and Britain.

Is there really a need for total union? The same acceptance of financial responsibility and respect of markets that might make full integration possible also allows close cooperation, unrestricted mobility, and highly developed specialization without formal federation. Indeed, any specific scheme to join the European nations into a sovereign unit would be unacceptable to many for a long time to come, and would thus reduce the openness so carefully built up. Moreover, who can confidently say that national reflexes would not prevail at the first serious difficulty, leading to cumulative disaggregation and possibly severe loss of what has already been achieved? These accomplishments, and others in prospect, are great aids to economic progress in all Europe, and there is in fact little inclination to sacrifice them for what might prove to be only the facade of union.

For the job remains economic growth. There is still too much individual poverty, too much community business to finish or to begin. And looking beyond the level of European incomes and the quality of her cities and recreation areas, the underdeveloped world needs resources that only a *growing* Europe will provide. Indeed, this points up perhaps the most compelling reason for retaining economic progress as a major social objective despite its restless and often brutal impact on societies. For Europe, as for the United States and other industrial countries, the alternative to growth is no longer poverty. But it is a stability that polarizes minds and attitudes around the protection of acquired positions. The result would be tension, suspicion, and strife at home, and a defensive and selfish attitude toward a poor world determined to close the gap. Europe has followed a long and arduous road toward the perspective of plenty, if not yet to its realization. It cannot refuse the lessons and some of the fruits of development to those who have so often been forgotten or oppressed contributors.

Bibliographical Note

I propose to do no more than mention a few books, in English, that I have particularly enjoyed. To attempt even a superficial coverage of the major topics on which the *Primer* touches would immediately swamp us. For many aspects, there are no works I can in good conscience recommend to the general reader as combining scholarship with readability. The references below are to paperback editions where they are available; more difficult or longer works are indicated by an asterisk (*).

General

Two brief books covering the long term are C. Cipolla's *Economic History of World Population* (Baltimore: Penguin Books, 1962) and R. Heilbroner's *The Making of Economic Society* (Englewood Cliffs, N.J.: Prentice-Hall, 1962). They differ in approach from the present *Primer* and from each other. W. W. Rostow's *Stages of Economic Growth* (Cambridge, England: Cambridge University Press, 1960) has influenced the language—and perhaps the substance—of debate about economic development. The reader wishing to delve deeper may find it wise to skip textbooks and go directly to the multivolume * *Cambridge Economic History of Europe,* still in the process of publication.

PART I *Preindustrial Europe*

For the Middle Ages, one can still read with profit some of H. Pirenne's work, although it is no longer up to date. *Medieval Cities* (Garden City, N. Y.: Anchor Books, 1956) and the *Economic and Social History of Medieval Europe* (New York: Harcourt Brace & World, n. d.) cover much the same ground. E. Power's *Medieval People* (New York: Barnes & Noble, 1963) is a series of delightful vignettes of everyday life. The

early medieval period has been provocatively interpreted by R. Latouche
in * *The Birth of the Western Economy* (New York: Harper & Row,
1966).
An excellent account of European trade and colonization is J. H. Parry's
The Establishment of the European Hegemony, 1415–1715 (New York:
Harper & Row, 1961). The special role of naval gunnery in this story is
the subject of C. Cipolla's *Guns, Sails, and Empires* (New York: Funk &
Wagnalls, 1967). R. H. Tawney's classic, * *Religion and the Rise of
Capitalism* (New York: Mentor Books, 1947), is still the best treatment
of the Protestant Ethic, although I like C. Hill's essay, "Protestantism
and Capitalism," in D. Landes (ed.), *The Rise of Capitalism* (New York:
Macmillan, 1966).

PART II *Economic Development in Europe*

Besides the little volume of readings edited by Landes, one can consult
B. Supple's collection of standard articles, * *The Experience of Economic Growth* (New York: Random House, 1963). An exciting panorama
of the first half of the period is E. J. Hobsbawm's *The Age of Revolution, 1789–1848* (New York: Mentor Books, 1964). For the ambitious
reader, the rise of industry is brilliantly analyzed by D. Landes in his
long essay, * "Technological Change and Industrial Development in
Western Europe, 1750–1914," in Volume VI of the above-mentioned
Cambridge Economic History of Europe.

PART III *Europe since 1914*

I know of no adequate summary of the interwar period. From an
abundant literature dealing with the postwar rejuvenation of Europe,
I would cite A. Maddison, * *Economic Growth in the West* (New York:
Twentieth Century Fund, 1964) as a source of quantitative data, and
recommend especially A. Shonfield's * *Modern Capitalism* (New York:
Oxford, 1965). U. W. Kitzinger's *Politics and Economics of European
Integration* (New York: Praeger, 1963) is good. Probably the best study
of a country, although it deals with more than the economic picture,
is *In Search of France,* by "six authors in search of a national character,"
headed by S. Hoffman (New York: Harper & Row, 1965). A recent survey
is M. M. Postan's *An Economic History of Western Europe, 1945–1964*
(New York: Barnes & Noble, 1967).

Index

Marxism, 159, 165, 183
Mass production, 100
Mechanization, 111, 123, 225
Mercantilism, 53–60, 175
  and capitalism, 160
Merchants, 31
  in Middle Ages, 31, 33–34
Metallurgy, 91–92
Metals, 40, 49
  precious, 54, 55
Middle Ages, 14–15, 62, 63
  capitalism in, 58
  Church in, 63–65
  land control in, 18–22
  rural economy in, 17–26
  trade in, 27–39
Middle class, 89, 104
Migrant labor, 213–214
Milan, 38
Minifundia, 153
Mining industry, 34
Mobility
  in developed economy, 75–76
  in international economy, 159
  regional, 126
Modernization, 37, 59
  in England, 79, 187
  in France, 127–131
  in Germany, 111, 112
Monetary reform, 204
Money, 101, 224–225
  during interwar period, 186–191
  and mercantilism, 55
  in Middle Ages, 32–33
Monopolies, 42, 43, 60
Moslems, 30
  and European trade growth, 46–49
Mussolini, Benito, 189, 195

Napoleon I, 118, 136, 139
Napoleon III, 127
Nationalism, 166, 229
  in Germany, 137
Nationalization, 192
Nazis, 196–197
New Economic Policy, 152, 189, 197
Nitrates, 142
North America, colonization of, 49, 50, 51, 52

North German Confederation, 137
Norway, trade of, 148

Ombudsman, 230
Open fields, 19, 25
Organization for Economic Co-operation and Development, 228
Owen, Robert, 104

"Parallel" markets, 178
Paris, 38, 117, 188
Paternalism, 42
Patriotism, 177–178
Peasants, 14, 122
  and enclosure, 81
  in manorial system, 20–22
Plan, le, 209, 230
Planning, economic, 179–180
  after World War II, 193, 209, 210, 216, 231
Population
  decline of, 37
  growth of, 37, 85, 120–121
Portugal, 49, 50, 219
Preindustrial economy, 61–68
Prices
  agricultural, 105
  and cartels, 142
  and colonial trade, 60
  and market economy, 41, 42
  rises in, 105
  stability of, 176, 207
Production, productivity, 40–41
  and investment, 106
  after World War II, 207
Profits, in booms, 105
Primogeniture, 89
Private initiative, 101
Proprietors, 80–81
Protection, tariff, 107, 117, 160
Protestant Ethic, 65–66, 153
Prussia, 136–137, 138, 213

Railroads
  in England, 93–94
  in Germany, 135, 138, 145
Reform Act of 1832, 97
Reformation, 62, 135

ABOUT THE AUTHOR

"And since it is observed, that the Generality of People, now a days, are unwilling either to commend or dispraise what they read, until they are in some measure informed who or what the Author of it is, whether he be *poor* or *rich*, *old* or *young*, a *Scollar* or a *Leather-Apron Man* . . ."

BENJAMIN FRANKLIN (*written at age 16*).

PAUL M. HOHENBERG *was born in Paris in 1933, and lived alternately there and in New York until he entered Cornell University. He studied chemical engineering at Cornell, international affairs at the Fletcher School of Law and Diplomacy, Tufts University, and took his doctorate in economics at M.I.T. In between, he worked as an engineer and taught modern languages. From 1963–1968 he was Assistant Professor of Economics at Stanford University and he is now Associate Professor of Economics at Cornell. Dr. Hohenberg is the author of* Chemicals in Western Europe, 1850–1914, *and has contributed to a number of professional journals.*

A NOTE ON THE TYPE

This book was set on the Linotype in BASKERVILLE, *a facsimile of the type designed by John Baskerville, Birmingham, England, in 1754. The original Baskerville type was one of the forerunners of the "modern" style of type faces. The Linotype copy was cut under the supervision of George W. Jones of London.*

Printed by Halliday Lithograph Corp., West Hanover, Mass. Bound by H. Wolff Book Mfg. Co., New York, N.Y.

Design by Leon Bolognese